WE LOVE YOU, BUT
YOU'RE GOING TO HELL

.

WE LOVE YOU, BUT YOU'RE GOING TO HELL

Christians and Homosexuality
Agree, Disagree, Take a Look

Dr. Kim O'Reilly

ELM HILL

A Division of
HarperCollins Christian Publishing

www.elmhillbooks.com

We Love You, But You're Going to Hell

Christians and Homosexuality Agree, Disagree, Take a Look

Published in Nashville, Tennessee, by Elm Hill, an imprint of Thomas Nelson. Elm Hill and Thomas Nelson are registered trademarks of HarperCollins Christian Publishing, Inc.

Elm Hill titles may be purchased in bulk for educational, business, fund-raising, or sales promotional use. For information, please e-mail SpecialMarkets@ThomasNelson.com.

Scripture quotations marked KJV are from the King James Version. Public domain.

Scripture quotations marked GNT are from the Good News Translation in Today's English Version—Second Edition. Copyright 1992 by American Bible Society. Used by permission.

Scripture quotations marked NET are from the NET Bible°. Copyright © 1996–2006 by Biblical Studies Press, L.L.C. http://netbible.com. All rights reserved.

Scripture quotations marked NIV are from the Holy Bible, New International Version°, NIV°. Copyright © 1973, 1978, 1984, 2011 by Biblica, Inc.° Used by permission of Zondervan. All rights reserved worldwide. www.zondervan.com. The "NIV" and "New International Version" are trademarks registered in the United States Patent and Trademark Office by Biblica, Inc.°

Scripture quotations marked NKJV are from the New King James Version°. © 1982 by Thomas Nelson. Used by permission. All rights reserved.

Scripture quotations marked NRSV are from New Revised Standard Version Bible. Copyright © 1989 National Council of the Churches of Christ in the United States of America. Used by permission. All rights reserved.

Library of Congress Cataloging-in-Publication Data

Library of Congress Control Number: 2018951437

ISBN 978-1-595557803 (Paperback)
ISBN 978-1-595558046 (Hardbound)
ISBN 978-1-595557919 (eBook)

DEDICATION

To my dear friend,

Fannie Beynon

1926 – 2017

Your love, prayers, support, humor, and wisdom
have meant the world to me. I will miss you.

Matthew 22:36–40 (KJV)

Master, which is the great commandment in the law?

Jesus said unto him, Thou shalt love the Lord thy God
with all thy heart, and with all thy soul,
and with all thy mind.

This is the first and great commandment.

And the second is like unto it,
Thou shalt love thy neighbour as thyself.

On these two commandments hang all the law
and the prophets.

CONTENTS

PROLOGUE

There is a growing divide between individuals and groups who hold different and contrasting beliefs about homosexuality. Dialogue is too often rare, and getting more so. People have little contact with those who hold differing opinions. Real progress can be made if we sit across the table, in the Church, or public meeting places to talk through our differences—in safety and respect. This book is an attempt to launch that dialogue.

CHAPTER 1

INTRODUCTION

I have written this book out of love and compassion. It is something that has been stirring in me, something that had to be birthed. Not just for my sake, but for the sake of so many gays and lesbians who identify themselves as Christian—or who would be drawn to Christianity if it were not for the condemnation they would receive. Homosexuals in the church have been given the option of ceasing to be gay, "choosing" to be heterosexual, remaining celibate, or going to Hell.

I am writing to those in the Church and asking you to consider that you may not have all of the information you need to draw the conclusion that your gay and lesbian church members, friends, or family are condemned to Hell by God. I would like to challenge you to read each of the chapters in my book; use it as a study guide in your Bible groups or adult Sunday school classes.

I am not condemning conservative Christians who believe and preach that homosexuality is an abomination. I understand the interpretation of the seven Scriptures used to condemn homosexuals, the history behind that condemnation, and the justification held by God-fearing, loving Christians. I invite those Christians to take the time to read my book. It is written in a fair-minded manner, without pointing fingers.

If you are convinced, as you pick up this book, that homosexuality is a sin and that homosexuals will go to Hell, it is worth your time to read it. Familiarize yourself with the Scriptures used to denounce homosexuality, look at what constitutes sexual orientation, learn how the Scriptures have wrongly been used to promote slavery and segregation, as well as to condemn homosexuals. Become aware of the inaccuracies behind the stereotypes of gays and lesbians, and discover how millions are adversely affected by the Church's judgment and condemnation.

If you are sure of your criticism and denunciation of homosexuality, still read this book to argue with it, challenge it, maybe change your mind on something, or confirm what you already believed going in. If you are certain that you know everything about sexual orientation and are qualified to condemn others based on your own knowledge, still read this book. It's worth the time to acquaint yourself with the Scriptures, challenge yourself, change your mind, and/or confirm that you have a solid foundation for your beliefs.

If you have people in your life who are gay or struggling with their sexuality because of the condemnation, it is worth your time to consider what this book has to say. Instead of handedly passing judgment, or demanding people change their sexual orientation, consider a more compassionate approach. Read the Scriptures and learn about sexual orientation. Leave the judgment to God. We won't know for certain this side of Heaven. If you err, err on the side of compassion.

What Brought Me to Write This Book

This was initially a response to Phil Robertson and his comments that went public in December 2013. I am a university professor who is very familiar with the Robertson family and enjoyed watching *Duck Dynasty*! While this credentials me with conservatives, my liberal friends have a hard time understanding my affection for the Robertson clan. I am uniquely positioned to respond, and my first draft was written as a letter to Phil Robertson:

Dear Phil,
    I read YOUR book Happy, Happy, Happy. *Now I ask that you read mine. Let me introduce myself...*

I have since decided to reframe the book so that it speaks to conservatives in general, the Robertsons included, and, of course, moderates and liberals. Phil Robertson had every right to voice his opinions based on his biblical beliefs. Since he had a public forum to do so, many on the Left criticized him. He has since emphasized his love for homosexuals, not hate. That's good, and hence the title for my book, *We Love You, But You're Going to Hell.*

There is no question that most conservative Christians advocate love, but in keeping with their interpretation of Scriptures they also advocate for repentance, changing to heterosexuality, or remaining single and celibate. These demands or expectations are based on seven Scriptures, confidence in an understanding of sexual orientation as only legitimately heterosexual, and certainty as to the will of God. The following Phil Robertson quotes demonstrate this:

> "We never, ever judge someone on who's going to heaven, hell. That's the Almighty's job. We just love 'em and give 'em the good news about Jesus—whether they're homosexuals, drunks, terrorists. We let God sort 'em out later."[1]
>
> "While Scriptures make it clear homosexual behavior is sin and comes under the judgment of God, it also indicates that those who are guilty of homosexual behavior or any other sin can be reconciled to God (2 Corinthians 5:17–21)."[2]
>
> "Jesus will take sins away, if you're a homosexual he'll take it away. If you're an adulterer, if you're a liar, what's the difference? If you break one sin you may as well break them all."[3]

Admirably, the message here is love. I agree that God is the judge, not the individual Christian. However, Robertson says homosexuality is a sin equivalent to alcoholism, lying, adultery. He believes that in repentance, homosexuality can be forgiven and changed to heterosexuality.

What This Book Is About

I want to address several of the Robertson statements. Yes, if God is the judge we should leave it to God. But many Christians have taken it upon themselves to speak for God and His judgment. With that comes the demand for repentance and changing sexual orientation. Asking for repentance assumes that there *is* a sin.

Chapter 4 looks at the seven Scriptures that are the basis on which to condemn homosexuality as a sin. Chapter 5 researches what constitutes sexual orientation. There is no evidence that sexual orientation can be changed; sexual behavior, yes—but not orientation or attraction. Chapter 6 addresses stereotypes and myths that have risen out of [mis] interpretation of the Scriptures. If stereotypes of homosexuals are not recognized, they will go unchallenged. Chapter 7 looks at how these stereotypes may be perpetuated by ministers and Churches.

With the belief that sexual orientation equates to heterosexuality, and homosexuality is sinful and deviant, conservative Christians want marriage to be reserved for heterosexual males and females. The debate has heated since the June 2015 Supreme Court decision. Chapter 8 will discuss all sides of this issue.

Religious freedom laws and court cases have risen out of differences over religious conviction and the rights of gays and lesbians to receive wedding-related services. Chapter 9 gives balanced coverage of this conflict.

The final two chapters identify problems and solutions. Why is it so important to look at Christians and homosexuality? Chapter 10 covers the damaging effects of conversion therapy, discrimination, Christian demands for changing orientation, and the self-loathing and even suicide that so sadly result when that cannot be accomplished. Family rejection, Church rejection, and leaving the Church are all consequences of not having the discussion my book covers and advocates.

Most importantly, Chapter 11 offers hope! Strategies, resources, and biblical references are given, moving from empathy and compassion to healing.

CHAPTER 2

My Story

I am a Christian, a minister's daughter, a university professor, and a lesbian. All labels that may conjure up
stereotypes and generalizations—as labels often do. I teach
about both the convenience of using labels and the down-
side in my classes. Labels can readily pinpoint identity and
tend to work well when chosen by the one self-identifying.
Even then, there are so many nuanced meanings that can be
applied.

Two of my labels might be associated with conservativ-
ism, two with liberalism. I am devout and Bible-believing,
my father was a fundamentalist minister, and I "profess" in a
liberal university. Many think that "Christian" and "lesbian"
can't be in the same sentence, let alone the same person.

I have been the exception to the rule. I grew up in a conservative Christian family, whom I love and respect. I've spent
a major part of my life on university campuses, obtaining

degrees or teaching others in that pursuit. Conservative is not a dirty word to me. Liberal is not, either. I straddle and live in both worlds without conflict or confusion. Now, my postman might be confused in delivering liberal and conservative materials to the same mailbox!

I started out early in life wanting to see or hear more than one side of issues or arguments. Although I didn't reference it as "critical thinking" then, it has remained central to my teaching and my relationships now. I think I came out of the womb asking questions, much to my parents' dismay. Questioning seems to be a common trait among teachers. Good thing, because it can serve us well in our profession.

I've also been a bridge-builder most of my life, looking for ways to understand and appreciate opposing or differing viewpoints. I am a moderate. In fact, I "moderate" in my classrooms. My students run the gamut of conservative, moderate, and liberal. All opinions are encouraged as long as they are presented respectfully and without personal attack. It takes finesse to facilitate discussions, to help students negotiate and share across differences. I am fortunate that I have had many years of practice, and it is what I find most rewarding. No political correctness, no censorship, no pressure, or finger-pointing. The skill of dialoguing across differences needs to be taken to the larger society, especially in today's polarizing environment. I always advocate for building bridges, not fences. That is my intention, and my hope, in writing this book.

My Early Years

I was born in Guyana, South America. My father was a Lutheran missionary who served several churches up and down the Berbice River in the interior of the Amazonian rain forest. I would tag along with him on occasion—for baptisms, funerals, and celebrations among the Amerindians. Congregants in the coastal villages were of African and East Indian (India) descent. My earliest memories were of trips to the market, paddling in dug-out canoes, and swimming in the Atlantic.

My arrival in New York City as a young girl was marked with some trepidation, as I didn't see any friendly faces. I had grown up with Africans and East Indians. My family was the only white family in that part of Guyana. I looked for familiar people of color and didn't see any. I saw a black woman at the top of the escalator in a New York City department store, ran up to her, jumped into her arms, and happily proclaimed that I had found a friend. Of course, through the eyes of a child, this story is oversimplified and only skin deep, but early memories shape us. The contrasting years of growing up in the Midwestern state of Iowa would do the same. I went from the Amazon to the Mississippi River. For a time, I couldn't relate to all of the white faces I saw until I adapted to my new culture.

It was religion and not race that would impact me as I grew up. As a minister's daughter, I found that differing ideologies and practices in the local denominations and religions stirred my interest. I couldn't understand why my

Catholic friends could not step into my Lutheran Church. When I asked them, they said that they only knew that it was wrong but not why. We visited Notre Dame University with my grandfather, who was also a Lutheran minister. A kind and gentle man, yet he refused to get out of the car to step on Catholic soil.

I wanted to understand why people believed what they believed. That's something I've carried over into my adulthood, especially around religion and homosexuality. In the sixth grade, I attempted to negotiate an agreement with my father to visit all of the churches in my hometown, so that I could learn more about them. While he was sympathetic to my request, he didn't think it would look good for his daughter to be seen in churches other than our own.

My father was asked to leave the Lutheran Church in the early 1970s, during a time that was referred to as the Charismatic or Jesus Movement. He had been preaching against infant baptism and several other Lutheran tenets. The Lutheran Church split with about half of the members joining my father in a "New Testament" church start-up.

My mother and father raised my three siblings and I to be conservative, to read the Bible, to have a personal relationship with God, and to attend church Sunday mornings and two evenings a week. We were taught about the end-times and given a deep understanding of sin, God's design and plan for our lives, and how to overcome the Adversary and remain hopeful in a world that would end some time during our lifetime.

I do not recall hearing direct preaching or discussion about homosexuality. In fact, I wasn't aware of the concept growing up or familiar with anyone who might be homosexual. I didn't have any preconceived ideas for or against. No struggles or conflicts. I got married shortly after graduating from high school. I gave birth to two beautiful boys in my early twenties. I was divorced at twenty-seven and raised my two sons through their teen years as a single parent.

It was when I started pursuing my teaching degree at the University of Iowa that my father and I began to openly disagree about politics or interpretations of the Bible. He would later say that attending the university caused me to become a lesbian. I pointed out to him that both he and my mother graduated from the same university, but that it didn't turn them into homosexuals. He didn't laugh about my comment at the time. Several years later, he did.

Coming Out to Myself

My process was not overnight. It was deeply personal and spiritual. In fact, I had for some time been looking at the Ninth Commandment from a different perspective than most. "Thou shalt not bear false witness against thy neighbor." I chose to focus that on myself, asking whether I was bearing false witness against myself AND others if I wasn't honest about who I was. My struggle was about integrity, being true to myself, looking at the Scriptures, talking to God.

I spent seven years in that endeavor. Nothing quick, nothing rash, nothing to prove. I've read the Bible several times since childhood. I reread and studied the Scriptures that my father and my Church quoted to prove that homosexuality was an abomination and a sin. I read every conservative anti-gay book, article, brochure that I could get my hands on. I also read all of the liberal, pro-gay material I could find. To be honest, I didn't find either side convincing. I questioned the harsh biblical interpretation, including historical and cultural contexts. On the other hand, much of the argumentation *for* the rightness of homosexuality was so secular and often anti-God or Bible. So, I prayed—dramatic as it sounds—unceasingly!

I have had a loving, personal relationship with Jesus almost all of my life. I talked with Him. I was sure of my salvation, my walk with God, how I walked through the world, how I was raising my sons. I felt assured of God's love and blessings. My life exhibited that. How then could I be asked by a loving God (according to the belief of my friends and family) to give up my sexuality? I saw loving, monogamous sexual expression as a gift from God. Was I really being asked to choose between God and my sexuality?

There are many who would answer that with a resounding yes. What a shame that others think they can know that so well for ME. Each of us has to come face-to-face with our Lord, our personal relationship, a reading of the Scriptures, and how we take that out into the world. What I found through it all was PEACE. Some may say that I found what I wanted, read the Scriptures through a lens that suited me, turned a blind eye, and deceived myself. Again, that is not for any of us to judge for another person. I would say peace cannot be fabricated. I have experienced that peace that passeth all understanding.

Coming Out to My Family

It was December 1995. All of my family were back in my hometown for the holidays. I had decided to come out to each of them individually. Admittedly, it would have taken a lot less emotional energy to tell them all at once. But, no regrets because I was able to have a one-on-one conversation with each of my siblings, in-laws, sons, mother, eventually working my way to my father. The joke became, "If Kim asks you out to lunch, don't go!"

I first told my sons, who were fourteen and sixteen, respectively, at the time. They were both happy for me and ready to go to a gay pride parade. I told my mother next. She was not surprised, expressed her biblical belief against it, but assured me that she loved me. She asked if I had been involved with a woman, because if I hadn't, I wasn't a homosexual. You had to be "practicing" to be a homosexual. I replied, "No involvement yet, but do you want me to call you when I become a lesbian?" Another occasion where one of my parents didn't laugh at the time, but laughed about it years later.

The emotions, questions, and responses from my family were varied. "Are you sure?" "Could it be a phase?" "I'm shocked." "I wondered." "I'm not surprised." "You became a lesbian because of a bad marriage." "Is it because you were molested?" "Why do you hate men?" "What you need is a good man." "I don't want you to influence my kids." "Are you the man or the woman in the relationship?"

The following is from a letter I received shortly after coming out. I have kept it to this day. It is well-meaning and written with love:

Kim,

I have thought about it, prayed about it, and anguished about it in my heart ever since you told me you are living a homosexual lifestyle.

I know that you know in your heart it is not natural, nor is it supported by God's Word. I do not judge you; that is for God to do. I also do not agree with your decision to live the way you do. I don't want to see you duped and deceived by the world's philosophies into believing such a blatant lie. I feel that in your quest for knowledge and enlightenment, you have overlooked and forgotten the basic tenets of biblical Christianity.

I sense that there are underlying layers of guilt, hurt, pain, bitterness, and shame that have driven you to this point in an attempt to find solace for your soul. Becoming a lesbian will not change the pain within. Only Jesus can mend broken hearts. Would you give Him the chance to mend yours? I'm not talking religion here. Religion is bankrupt. I'm talking about a personal relationship with Jesus Christ Himself.

I've included the specifics of much of this letter because my gay and lesbian readers have probably received similar notes. Perhaps not even as loving and kind. Any reader who believes homosexuality is a sin could have written this with sincerity and conviction. I still have a copy of what I wrote in response.

Referencing the first paragraph: "Living a homosexual lifestyle"

> *What lifestyle? By referring to it as a lifestyle denigrates and diminishes my life, my relationship with the woman I love. I am still the same daughter, sister, niece, friend, teacher, student, and mother. My lifestyle, going to school, grocery shopping, raising my sons hasn't changed.*

Referencing the second paragraph: "I know that you know in your heart it is not natural."

> *You cannot know that for me. You've placed onto me your feelings about it not being natural. It is natural for me.*

"It is not supported by God's Word."

> *I believe it is supported by God's Word and would like to share those Scriptures. Many of the same Scriptures you've shared with me.*

"In your quest for knowledge and enlightenment, you have overlooked and forgotten the basic tenets of biblical Christianity."

You said you aren't judging me. That is very judgmental. My biblical beliefs remain intact. I have not strayed from those tenets. We disagree on homosexuality not on salvation, forgiveness, the life of Jesus.

Referencing the third paragraph: "I sense that there are underlying layers of guilt, hurt, pain, bitterness, and shame that have driven you to this point in an attempt to find solace for your soul."

To say that I'm full of pain and anguish is presumptive—projecting what YOU feel about this onto me. The decision to come out wasn't an overnight decision. I am not full of guilt, hurt, and pain. I am very much at peace. You don't "become" a heterosexual or a lesbian in response to something.

"Jesus can mend broken hearts. I'm talking about a personal relationship with Jesus Christ Himself."

I agree, Jesus can absolutely mend broken hearts and my personal relationship with Christ is central to who I am and how I express myself in this world.

This letter was written by someone important to me; however, not my father. From the time I was young, my dad and I were close. We would often argue or challenge each other, but usually we agreed to disagree. I would like to share how my coming out impacted our relationship.

The Journey with My Father

By the time I told my father that holiday, he had already heard about it from a family friend—weeks before. My hometown in Middle America was small, a town of 22,000 souls, and I had recently begun dating a well-known local businesswoman.

My father sat on the board of an antigay religious group the year before, spearheading an opposition to a human rights ordinance. The ordinance stated that people could not be discriminated against in housing, education, and employment based upon their sexual orientation. My father preached that citizens would be forced to hire or work with homosexuals against their own belief and comfort level. An example given: a straight fireman being forced to sleep next to a gay man. He might be subjected to harassment or molestation. Even at that time—a year before coming out—I challenged my father, saying that there are laws in place that protect against harassment and molestation, and that those are unfair stereotypes attributed to homosexuals. The woman who would later become my partner spoke on behalf of the ordinance at many city council meetings. With heavy antigay positioning, it did not pass.

Needless to say, my coming out, and also dating a woman who had publicly opposed my father, did not initially bode well for our relationship. He wanted to go toe-to-toe with me on the Scriptures. I have always had a deep respect for my dad, his knowledge, and his study of the Bible. He was faithful, true to his belief and his reading of the Word. I understood that. We went over each Scripture. This time, he wouldn't agree to disagree. He didn't speak to me over the next six months. It was my mother who finally spoke up and told him that, regardless of his beliefs, I was still his daughter.

We were cordial; eventually there was no tension, and my partner was accepted at family events. Still, my father would take me aside on occasion to share materials such as *Is the Homosexual Sick or Sinful?* by Dr. Jack Hyles. An excerpt from this booklet says: "The question is raised as to whether the homosexual is a sinner or a patient; whether he is sick or sinful, whether he should be pitied or scolded, whether he should go to a doctor for treatment or a preacher for conversion, whether he needs the medical journal or the Bible, whether he needs counseling or repentance, whether he needs a clinic or a church. The Scripture is plain in answering, 'Is the homosexual sick or sinful?'"[1]

After moving away to take my first university position, my dad wrote letters emphasizing that homosexuality was an abomination to God, was punishable by death in the Old Testament, and can be cured. He continued to write and send materials over the years—all in love, with concern, and urging me to change.

He wrote beautiful letters. I have one of his last handwritten letters in front of me now.

I want you to know, Kim, that the life you chose to live, first with ___, and now with ___ has not in any way affected my love for you, or my love and respect for ___. She is looked upon by me as my fifth daughter. I honor and respect you *and am so proud of you for all that you have accomplished and often with the odds against you.*

Kim, you know and have always known where I stand, biblically, concerning the life you have chosen to live with a woman as your helpmate. I can't move from that position after studying His Word in both the original Hebrew of the Old Testament and the Greek of the New Testament. Because of my position I could not offer my approval or congratulations upon hearing that you and ___ flew to Vancouver, BC, to exchange vows during a same-sex ceremony. Don't ever expect me to congratulate you. However, always expect me to love you, accept you and treasure you as my daughter... my very favorite university professor.

A deep love between us—the paradox: he loved and respected me, but didn't approve of "my homosexuality," and feared that I was going to Hell. Walking and talking through that is what brings me to writing this book. Many gays find themselves in the same dilemma, but haven't experienced that love or any degree of acceptance from their parents or family members. The journey with my father culminated in a meaningful encounter the last time we were together, a few months before he unexpectedly passed away.

The two of us were at his sister's home in Oregon. My father and I carved out a day to visit his old stomping grounds, where he grew up. He wanted to talk before we left the house. He had been thinking about it for some time and wanted me to know that he had wrongly been judgmental of me. That he needed to leave any judgment with God. He tearfully asked me to forgive him.

I remember so fondly that day—for so many reasons. Here was my father, a conservative fundamentalist minister of seventy-eight years, asking that I forgive him for judging me. His beliefs and interpretation of the Bible remained intact. He didn't want to come down on the wrong side of judgment, or as judging, and thankfully shared that with me while he was still alive.

I know I am blessed to have had that kind of relationship with my father. I am also fortunate that I've had a loving, personal relationship with God. I didn't struggle or take on the disapproval and condemnation I received from my father and others over the years—a disapproval that was well-meaning and expressed in love, but nonetheless a disapproval. It is a double-edged sword—love and condemnation. *We love you, but you're going to Hell.* I want to sincerely, and without pointing fingers, address that dichotomy throughout this book. So many Christian gays and lesbians have been damaged by that well-meaning love—expected to change their orientation, leave loving relationships, remain celibate and single, never to marry.

It all starts with biblical interpretation.

In the next chapter, let's first look at Scriptures that were wrongly used for centuries to promote and maintain slavery and segregation.

CHAPTER 3

SCRIPTURES USED TO PROMOTE SLAVERY AND SEGREGATION

"Slavery was established by decree of Almighty God...it is sanctioned in the Bible, in both Testaments, from Genesis to Revelations...it has existed in all ages, has been found among the people of the highest civilization, and in nations of the highest proficiency in the arts"[1]

—JEFFERSON DAVIS, PRESIDENT OF THE
CONFEDERATE STATES

"There is not one verse in the Bible inhibiting slavery, but many regulating it. It is not then, we conclude, immoral."[2]

—REV. ALEXANDER CAMPBELL

From the founding of our nation and the establishment of the slave trade, the majority of politicians and ministers referenced the Bible in their defense of slavery. Biblical passages recognized, controlled, and regulated the practice. It was said that the Apostle Paul had every opportunity to write in one of his Epistles that human slavery was profoundly evil. His letter to Philemon referencing his escaped slave would have been an ideal opportunity to vilify slavery. But he did not write a word criticizing the institution. For hundreds of years, that was taken as approval and promotion of slavery.

Jesus could have condemned the practice. He might have done so, but there is no record of him having said anything negative about slavery. In the absence of condemnation, and acceptance of the practice throughout the Bible, slavery was considered the norm, a God-given right to slaveholders.

It is obvious to most now that the Bible was misused and misinterpreted to promote the interests of slave owners. Over time, enough people began to criticize the Scriptures and question the interpretations in the face of such an ugly and abusive practice as owning fellow human beings. Scriptures were effectively used for centuries to justify and encourage keeping slaves in bondage.

The Christian Church's main justification for slavery was based on Genesis 9:25–27. A worldwide flood left eight human survivors: Noah, his wife, his three sons, and their wives. Noah's son Ham had accidentally seen "the nakedness of his father." Ham's descendants were cursed by Noah. Christians traditionally believed that Ham and his son Canaan had settled in Africa. The dark skin of Africans was associated with this curse of Ham. Thus, enslavement of Africans became religiously justifiable upon the reading of this Scripture in Genesis.

Cursing an entire race into slavery was considered acceptable because it was thought to be in the Bible. American slave owners, almost all of whom were Christians, felt they were carrying out God's plan by buying and holding slaves. Challenging this interpretation was paramount to being ungodly and anti-Christian. The early abolitionists were accused of being against the Church, unpatriotic, and even anti-American. Slavery was seen as an American institution that brought economic prosperity and stability. To question it or consider it immoral ran contrary to commonly-held biblical beliefs.

In 1851, writer Josiah Priest published a book that was widely cited by slave owners. In *Bible Defence of Slavery; And Origin Fortunes, and History of the Negro Race*, he wrote:

"If God appointed the race of Ham judicially to slavery, and it were a heinous sin to enslave one, or all the race, how then is the appointment of God to go into effect? God does never sanction sin, nor call for the commission of moral evil to forward any of his purposes; wherefore we come to the conclusion, that it is not sinful to enslave the negro race, providing it is done in a tender, fatherly and thoughtful manner."[3]

This rationale proved to be a conundrum for questioning Christians who abhorred slavery, but were not able to shore their personal convictions against such an argument. The conclusion, over time, by a growing number of Christians was that the *interpretation* of Genesis 9:25–27 was wrong. That Ham seeing Noah in his nakedness and any consequent curse should not be interpreted as God condoning or commanding slavery. Therefore, enslaving humans could be seen as wrong. The debate over biblical understanding became heated. Pro-slavery advocates went a step further to emphasize that "tender, fatherly, thoughtful" enslavement provided further justification.

Numerous other Scriptures, in addition to the Genesis account, were brought out vociferously in support of slavery, especially in the last days before it was finally outlawed in 1865.

> "As the eyes of slaves look to the hand of their master...
> so our eyes look to the Lord our God..."
> (Psalm 123:2) (NIV)

> "Slaves, obey your earthly masters with respect and
> fear... Masters, treat your slaves in the same way..."
> (Ephesians 6:5, 9) (NIV)

> "Slaves, obey your earthly masters in everything..."
> (Colossians 3:22) (NIV)

"Masters, provide your slaves with what is right and fair, because you know that you also have a Master in heaven."

(Colossians 4:1) (NIV)

"Teach slaves to be subject to their masters in everything, to try to please them, not to talk back to them."

(Titus 2:9) (NIV)

"Slaves, in reverent fear of God, submit yourselves to your masters not only to those who are good and considerate, but also to those who are harsh."

(I Peter 2:18) (NIV)

Slave owners often read these verses to slaves during the worship services they allowed and controlled. These Scriptures were used to encourage proper attitude and obedience. The irony is that slaves adopted the very religion that preached the rightness of their enslavement. Yet in the midst, slaves *adapted* Christianity and the Word of God to include themselves—simultaneous interpretations of the same Bible. One interpretation saw slavery as natural and God's will, the other saw God's grace and the promise of freedom, evidence that multiple biblical interpretations can and do coexist.

The Bible and Segregation

In the century following the passing of the Thirteenth Amendment, there remained an insistence that the Bible advocated for the subjugation and lower status of African-Americans. The rhetoric changed from slavery as the will of God to separation of the races as God's will. Scriptures continued to be used in much the same way they had been used to justify slavery. After the Civil War, the focus was on how God meant the races to be separate and within a hierarchy.

The 1896 Supreme Court decision, *Plessy v Ferguson*, gave a green light to segregationists. Although the basis for the decision was not directly drawn from the Bible, it reinforced the Southern Christians' belief that the Scriptures promoted racial segregation. Homer Plessy, seven-eighths European descent and one-eighth African descent, was classified as "black" and was required to sit at the back of the train, in the "colored" car. He was arrested for refusing to leave the "white" section. The Supreme Court ruled in favor of the state of Louisiana in a "Separate but Equal" clause. As long as separate black and white facilities—drinking fountains, seating, schools—were equal, state segregation laws were upheld as legal. It has since been demonstrated throughout U.S. history that separate facilities were never equal.

A Georgia Supreme Court ruling prior to this exemplifies the belief that the Bible upholds segregation and that it is God's natural law.

"Moral or social equality between the different races does not in fact exist, and never can. The God of nature made it otherwise, and no human law can produce it, and no human tribunal can enforce it. There are gradations and classes throughout the universe. From the tallest archangel in Heaven, down to the meanest reptile on earth, moral and social inequalities exist, and must continue to exist throughout all eternity."[4]

Those Christians who believed segregation was God's natural law were outraged with the 1954 Supreme Court decision that overturned *Plessy v Ferguson*. There were claims that God would turn His back on the nation if segregation was dismantled. Accusations of communism and atheism were lobbed against integrationists. "No Race Mixing" signs could be seen at each of the sites of the schools first integrated—in Topeka, KS; Little Rock, AR; and Oxford, MS.

The no-race mixing sentiment carried over into religious beliefs about interracial marriage and laws. A Supreme Court decision in 1967 legalized marriage between all races nationwide. Sixteen states in the South and Midwest still had laws that enforced criminal punishment for mixed-race couples. Citing the Bible, God's will, and states' rights, many of those states refused to honor interracial marriage and saw it as a defeat for Christianity. An argument from a Virginia judge at the time states:

"Almighty God created the races white, black, yellow, Malay and red, and he placed them on separate continents. But for the interference with his arrangement there would be no cause for such marriages. The fact that he separated the races shows that he did not intend for the races to mix."[5]

Hundreds of years of biblical interpretation and state laws in the U.S. supported slavery and segregation. Thankfully, those interpretations were eventually challenged and state laws were changed. Similarly, hundreds of years of biblical interpretation and state laws have condemned and punished homosexuals.

The following chapter looks at those Scriptures, the commonly-held beliefs around them, and offers alternate viewpoints.

CHAPTER 4

SCRIPTURES USED TO CONDEMN HOMOSEXUALS

"It is unfortunate that when you quote the Bible people get upset about one particular sin that always seems to get a lot of attention. But sometimes the Bible is going to rub folks the wrong way."

"The Bible is crystal clear about homosexuality."

"God judges those who practice homosexuality."

"Homosexuals will face the wrath of God. It's what the Holy Bible says—period!"

"God's word is final."

There are seven Scriptures commonly cited in reference to homosexuality. As evidenced by these opening quotes, the traditional Christian approach to homosexuality has been to view it as a sin, based on the biblical witness and on Christian tradition. At the surface of this observation, there can be little debate. The Bible nowhere condones same-sex relations and, in a few places, explicitly censures them. The question though is: "What constitutes the *sin* of same-sex relations?" Embracing pagan and idolatrous practices, acts of dominance and violence, and going against ancient notions of human nature are denounced in the scriptural passages.

Biblical scribes, or anyone else writing in those centuries, had no idea or concept of homosexual orientation—a lifelong attraction, fixed early, toward people of the same sex. There was no word for it until a German psychologist, Karoly Maria Benkert, coined the term in 1869. It comes from the Greek word *homos*, meaning the same. The word itself did not appear in the English Bible until 1946.

This chapter will look at each of the seven Scriptures that have reinforced beliefs about the immorality of same-sex expression. It is clear that understanding of sexual orientation today is different from that of the biblical writers. Much more is known in the twenty-first century.

Heterosexuality comprises the majority in human populations, and so has been considered the *norm* across cultures and history. Heterosexuality as the norm would naturally be assumed throughout the Bible. Genesis 1 and 2 tells the story of Adam and Eve. Detractors will point out that it was not Adam and Steve. It makes sense that the Genesis accounts detail the events of the first male and female who began humanity. The Genesis story emphasizes procreation. It would not be expected otherwise. That emphasis does not negate or condemn homosexuality. It is true that homosexuals cannot procreate. Relationships do not require procreation in order to be legitimate. Childless heterosexual couples are not diminished because they have not, or cannot, bring children into the world.

The creation story has been used to criticize homosexuality because the first two human beings were heterosexual and procreated. Other cited Scriptures *do* condemn same-sex acts that violate ancient Hebrew purity and holiness codes. There is further denunciation of homosexual prostitution, acts of idolatry, and pederasty (adult males sexually exploiting boys). Scriptural condemnation is also evident for similar *heterosexual* acts, those that violate holiness codes, commercial sex, heterosexual temple prostitution, and sexual misuse of minors.

Genesis 19:1–29
(Sodom and Gomorrah)

The story of Sodom and Gomorrah is perhaps the most famous instance in Scripture where homosexuality is seen to be condemned. The term *sodomy*, still in the vernacular, derogatorily references male homosexuals. God announced judgment on Sodom and Gomorrah in Genesis 18. He sent angels to Sodom, where Abraham's nephew, Lot, persuaded them to stay in his home. Genesis 19 records that "all the people from every quarter" surrounded Lot's house, demanding the release of his visitors so that "we might know them." *Know* (Hebrew: *yadha*) means to have thorough knowledge of; two common interpretations include examining credentials or to have sexual intercourse. If the latter, it would be a clear case of attempted gang rape. It was not just a group of men, but the whole community that converged outside of Lot's house. He refused their demands and, in a perverse gesture of hospitality, offered his two daughters to the mob. Judges 19:22–24 is almost identical to the Sodom account but focuses on the town of Gibeah. In Sodom, the two daughters were not actually delivered. But in Gibeah, the female who was offered was subsequently raped and died.

What was the sin of Sodom? Ezekiel 16:48–50 (NIV) states it clearly: "This was the sin of your sister Sodom: she and her daughters were arrogant, overfed and unconcerned; they did not help the poor and needy." There are many other passages in the Bible that mention Sodom—Ecclesiastes 16, Isaiah 1, and Jeremiah 23; Jesus' words in Matthew 11:24 and Luke 10:10–12.

The sins most attributed to Sodom are selfishness, arrogance, and inhospitality. Josephus wrote about Sodom in 96 AD, "Indignant at this conduct, God accordingly resolved to chastise them for their arrogance."[1] It was not until St. Augustine's *Confessions* in 400 CE that Sodom's sin was solely identified with homosexuality.

Leviticus 18:22 and 20:13
(Holiness Codes)

"You shall not lie with a male as with a woman; it is an abomination."

"If a man lies with a male as with a woman, both of them have committed an abomination; they shall be put to death; their blood is upon them." (KJV)

Many evangelical leaders suggest that these two Old Testament passages are the most explicit in their condemnation of homosexuals. In fact, these verses served as the foundation for European laws that mandated the death penalty for homosexuals until the end of the eighteenth century.

The statements in both Scriptures are clear, but the context and application are not. Holiness Codes were laws aimed at keeping the Hebrew people pure and separate from other cultures—foundational commandments for nation-building and for survival. Both Levitical passages reference only male-to-male sexual acts. Emphasis was placed on propagation for a struggling nation. Wasted "seed" between males and in masturbation were prohibited.

Taking these Holiness Codes literally in the twenty-first century is not advocated by Christians—neither are stoning adulterers or those who curse their parents; designating foods such as shellfish, pork, rabbit as unclean; or punishing masturbation. Christian tradition has viewed the purity concerns and regulations in Leviticus as irrelevant. Yet, these Scriptures are still cited to condemn homosexuals. Other sexual behaviors that are considered inherently immoral are mentioned elsewhere in the Old Testament; male "homosexuality" is not mentioned again. The next Scripture used to denounce homosexuals is found in the New Testament.

Romans 1:26–27

"For this reason, God gave them up to vile passions. For even their women exchanged the natural use for what is against nature. And likewise also the men, leaving the natural use of the woman, burned in their lust toward one another, men with men committing what is shameful, and receiving in themselves the penalty of their error which was due." (NKJV)

Most New Testament books, including the four Gospels, are completely silent on same-sex acts. Paul has the most to say about sexuality. Essentially, he encouraged mutuality and reciprocity, and he assumed that there was a committed monogamous relational context for all sexual expressions. Obviously, Paul took relations between men and women as normative. Paul didn't write about homosexuality in Romans, neither about homosexuality or homoeroticism as *he* might have understood it, nor about homosexuality as we *now* understand it. He described what happens to followers of Christ who turned to idols and to other religions—rebellion against God and its consequences.[2]

Paul knew only of exploitive forms of homoerotic

expression, particularly pederasty and male prostitution. There *are* forms of homosexuality where the relationship is one of mutuality, commitment, and care. Paul saw all forms of homoeroticism as expressions of insatiable lust. There *are* homosexual relationships where the sexual aspect is no more or less obsessive than in comparable heterosexual relationships. Paul assumed that all homoerotic relations were a consequence of Gentile idolatry. There *are* gay and lesbian Christians who faithfully and genuinely worship Christ.

Scholars do not agree on what sort of relationships Paul wrote about in Romans 1. He used the Greek word *para physin* to describe women and men violating gender roles. He referenced men taking the traditionally submissive female role sexually and women the dominant. *Para physin* has commonly been translated to mean "unnatural." A heterosexual involved in homosexual acts would be seen as contradicting one's own nature. It is also going against one's own nature when homosexuals are expected to engage in heterosexual relations.

Although there was no concept of sexual orientation when Paul wrote to the Romans, male-female sexuality was considered the norm. Paul saw opposite-sex relations as *natural* and same-sex as *unnatural*. Non-procreative sex was also considered *unnatural* because it elevated physical pleasure over the spiritual. Homosexuality, masturbation, oral sex, and sex with birth control were all equally unnatural in this sense. We don't necessarily adhere to those prescriptions of what is *natural* today.

For Paul, and many Church leaders over the next centuries,

the "natural order" was that men should dominate women. This is what Paul meant by "unnatural": when women are active, or dominant, and men are passive. This is also why males having sex with males was considered unnatural. It involves a man taking the woman's role. In Paul's time, as in many cultures today, the real offense of male homosexuality is not just that two men are involved, but that one man is taking on the "female" role. Paul saw these acts by heterosexuals as "vile affections" because they violated the rigidly prescribed power roles of the two sexes.

Romans 1:26–31 (KJV) also lists other activities and attitudes as wicked among the rebellious. Paul said they are "filled with unrighteousness, fornication, wickedness, covetousness, maliciousness," "envy, murder," and "backbiters, haters of God, despiteful, proud, boasters." This raises some questions about the heavy emphasis the Church has placed on homosexuality, based on this passage in Romans. Church leaders have not voted to censure backbiting or gossip at conventions. Pastors have not been denied appointments because of boastfulness. Yet, many Christian denominations over time have gathered to condemn homosexual members and leaders in their fold.

In the second of the three passages of Paul on this subject, he wrote strongly of his disapproval of sexual acts that are exploitive, like harming a partner or ignoring his or her worth as a child of God. Few would disagree with his condemnation of such behavior, whether by homosexuals or heterosexuals.

I Corinthians 6:9–10

"Do you not know that wrongdoers will not inherit the kingdom of God? Do not be deceived! Fornicators, idolaters, adulterers, *male prostitutes*, *sodomites*, thieves, the greedy, drunkards, revilers, robbers— none of these will inherit the kingdom of God." (NSRV)

Understanding the background of Paul's teachings in Romans helps to make sense of the two remaining Pauline passages that mention same-sex behavior: I Corinthians 6:9–10 and I Timothy 1:9–10. Paul's letter to the Corinthians contains a list of behaviors that are incompatible with inheriting the kingdom of God. Some modern translations include *effeminate* in place of male prostitutes and *homosexuals* in place of sodomites. The words used in the original Greek texts are *malakoi* and *arsenokoitai*.

Malakoi is translated in the King James Bible as effeminate. It translates as "soft," most likely referring to someone who lacks discipline or moral control. The word is used elsewhere in the New Testament, but never as a reference to sexuality. *Arsenokoitai* is only found in this passage and in I Timothy 1:10. It is difficult to translate as it is very rarely found in Greek literature. It is derived from two Greek words, one meaning "male" and the other "beds"; literally translated as male-bedders.[3] The larger context of I Corinthians 6 shows Paul extremely concerned with prostitution. Christians were joining themselves to temple prostitutes in Corinth, the center of Aphrodite worship. This would indicate that Paul was concerned with male temple prostitution.

The difficulty in translating *malakoi* or *arsenokoitai* demonstrates that it is not as clear-cut a condemnation of homosexuality, as many evangelical leaders believe. In fact, it has little to do with homosexual orientation, but rather male prostitution and pederasty.

Examples of the range of translations for *malakoi* over the centuries are Tyndale (1525) as *weaklings*, King James (1611) as *effeminate*, New American (1970) as *boy pros-titutes*, New Jerusalem (1973) as *self-indulgent*, New International (1978) and New Revised Standard (1990) as *male prostitutes*.[4]

Arsenokoitai translates in the King James Version (1611) as *abusers of themselves with mankind*; in the Jerusalem Bible (French, 1966): *men with infamous desires*; the Jerusalem Bible (German, 1968): *boy molesters*; the New American Bible (1970): *homosexuals*; the New International Version (1978): *homosexual offenders*; and the New Revised Standard Version (1990): *sodomites*. Prior to ever being translated as homosexual, *arsenokoitai* was interpreted by early Christian writers as a reference to child molestation and anal sex between husbands and wives.[5]

I Timothy 1:9–10

"This means understanding that the law is laid down not for the innocent but lawless and disobedient, for the godless and sinful, for the unholy and profane, for those who kill their father or mother, for murderers, fornicators, *sodomites*, slave traders, liars, perjurers, and whatever else is contrary to the sound teaching." (NRSV)

As in the I Corinthians passage, the Greek word translated as sodomite is *arsenokoitai*, meaning abusers of themselves, boy molesters, male prostitutes, or homosexuals. The Greek word *pornois* translates as *fornicator* and can also refer to male prostitutes. Fornicators, sodomites, and slave traders may collectively reference the sex trade that developed in the Roman Empire of that day, referring to the customers, victims, and profiteers who participated in human trafficking.

Jude 1:7

"Even as Sodom and Gomorrah, and the cities about them in like manner, giving themselves over to fornication, and going after strange flesh, are set forth for an example, suffering the vengeance of eternal fire." (KJV)

As discussed earlier in this chapter, the sin of Sodom and Gomorrah was attempted gang rape, inhospitality, and arrogance. *Strange flesh* alludes to having sex with angels. Jude didn't say anything about males having sex with males or females having sex with females. There is no reason to associate this Scripture with homosexuality.[6]

Scriptural Overview

The Bible says very little about homosexuality. The relevant passages address exploitive forms of homoerotic sexual practice. Genesis 19:5 is about gang rape and inhospitality. The Holiness Codes of Leviticus 18:22 and 20:13 seek to preserve the male "seed" for propagation and survival. Romans 1:26–27 condemns men and women who violate sexual gender roles, male prostitution, and pederasty. In I Corinthians 6:9–10 and I Timothy 1:9–10, the translations of *malakoi* and *arsenokoitai* are varied. Most interpretations refer to male prostitution and pederasty. Jude wrote about the sin of Sodom and Gomorrah: gang rape and inhospitality, and strange flesh (sex with angels).

The rarity with which Paul discussed any form of same-sex behavior, and the ambiguity in references attributed to him, make it dubious to conclude a sure position in the New Testament on homosexuality, especially in the context of loving, responsible relationships.

The Teachings of Jesus

None of the four Gospels report that Jesus said anything about homosexuality. This does not necessarily mean that he had no opinion on the subject. But it is fair to suggest that neither he nor his biographers considered it a very important concern.

Some say that since Jesus upheld the law, his silence on

homosexuality indicates his acceptance of the teachings of Hebrew Scripture in Genesis and Leviticus, and therefore, he was against homosexuality. However, his references to Sodom in Matthew 11:24 and Luke 10:10–12 emphasized the sins of selfishness, arrogance, and inhospitality—not homosexuality. "Whoever shall not receive you, nor hear your words, when ye depart out of that house or city, shake off the dust of your feet. Verily, I say unto you, it shall be more tolerable for the land of Sodom and Gomorrah in the day of judgment, than for that city." (KJV)

Jesus said nothing directly about homosexuality—for or against it. When he did condemn human behavior, it was likely to be the sins of self-righteousness and arrogance. If he never mentioned homosexual acts, he certainly spoke often of the hardness of heart of religious insiders. He clearly advocated that religious institutions leave the business of judging to God.

It is also apparent that what we mean by the term "homosexuality" in the early twenty-first century is different from what is alluded in the seven Scriptures we just covered. The writers of the Old and New Testaments did not have any notion of heterosexual and homosexual orientations.

The next chapter will examine what constitutes sexual orientation.

CHAPTER 5

SEXUAL ORIENTATION

"The first step to repentance is recognizing sin for what it is and rejecting deceptive attempts to sanitize it by calling it something else, i.e., choice, sexual orientation."

"God doesn't make mistakes. Humans do. God doesn't make one gay. They make that choice on their own."

"It's a fact that homosexuality is a choice. It has a cause—Satan."

These statements are straightforward and adamant in the claim that homosexuality is a sin, a choice, and caused by Satan. Chapter 4 looked closely at the Scriptures used to condemn homosexuality as a sin. I argue that it is not a sin, and that it is unfair to make such accusation based on seven Scriptures about male prostitution, pederasty, and pagan sex rituals. I am not asking anyone to deny their beliefs, but to consider that they may not have enough information about homosexuality to determine that it is a choice and caused by Satan.

Why should our attitudes change now, when, for hundreds of years, homosexuality was reviled by so many religious authorities? A similar question was asked over a century ago about the Bible, slavery, and religious authority. Many began to question the interpretation of Scriptures that were used to support slavery. Likewise, now, the Scriptures that are used to condemn homosexuality. New information and thinking came to light about natural law, human rights, and dignity. Christians could no longer justify owning slaves. New information about sexual orientation, emotional and physical attraction, and identity emerged after over a century of research. It is my hope that Christians will no longer justify condemning homosexuals. What is the cause of homosexuality? Is it a choice? Can it be changed? The answers to these questions hinge on an understanding of sexual orientation.

Sexual Orientation Is Not Just About Sex

The American Psychological Association defines sexual orientation as an enduring pattern of emotional, romantic, and/or sexual attraction to men, women, or both sexes. Sexual orientation also refers to a person's sense of identity, based on those attractions, related behaviors, and membership in a community of others who share those attractions. Research over several decades has demonstrated that sexual orientation ranges along a continuum, from exclusive attraction to the opposite sex to exclusive attraction to the same sex. Orientation is usually discussed in terms of three categories along that continuum: heterosexual, homosexual, and bisexual.

Viewing homosexuality as a sin reduces lesbians and gays down to a sex act, as if that alone defines sexuality. The label or assumption of sin denies any emotional component, any capacity to feel real love or show genuine affection. Sexual orientation is also about intimate personal relationships that meet deeply felt needs for love, attachment, and intimacy. Heterosexuals know that the physical act of sex isn't the totality of their sexuality, that it is also about affection and companionship, and the desire to love and be loved. That is true for homosexuals as well.

We Don't Know the Cause of Sexual Orientation

There is no consensus among scientists and as to what causes sexual orientation. We don't know why people are heterosexual, bisexual, or homosexual. More than one hundred theories have been proposed by scientists and religious leaders. Those theories explaining the cause of homosexuality range from biology, genetics, sex hormones, upbringing, mothers, fathers, siblings, birth order, Satan, God, sin, deception, peer pressure, disco music, bad marriages, mental illness, and immaturity. The list goes on. No single scientific theory fits all the evidence or holds up under the rigors of peer review by other researchers.

No single hypothesis can explain why one person's romantic daydreams center on the opposite sex, while another's focuses on the same sex. Or even within an orientation, why some are attracted to blonds, redheads, brunettes, or a particular personality type. So many songs and books have been devoted to the *mysteries* of love and attraction.

Within the last twenty years, considerable evidence points toward a biological basis for homosexuality. While that can take the argument away from choice, many gays worry that if a "homosexual gene" is discovered, it could lead to some advocating for the eradication of that gene. Much research has examined the possible genetic, hormonal, developmental, social, and cultural influences on sexual orientation, but no findings have emerged that permit scientists to conclude that sexual orientation is determined by any one factor. *Nature* and *nurture* both play complex roles.

The cause of heterosexuality or homosexuality cannot be pinpointed. Why is the question about what causes homosexuality being asked? For those who are convinced that the Bible condemns homosexuality, the cause is important. If it is sin, or demonic, or a mental illness, or a choice—rather than genetic, or from God, or fixed at birth, or an unknown combination of factors—then demands can still be made for homosexuals to change their orientation.

We Cannot Choose Our Sexual Orientation

Someone who is gay can choose to *behave* heterosexually, but behavior is not the same as orientation. Many researchers report that sexual orientation is fixed at birth, and that most people experience little or no sense of choice about it. Bisexuality is often confused with choice since it is an orientation where someone is attracted to both sexes. They "choose" to be involved with the same sex or opposite sex. Sigmund Freud believed that human beings are born bisexual and can move along a continuum of sexuality. After the turn of the century, this contributed to the belief that homosexuals could choose heterosexuality.

Many Christians who condemn homosexuality argue that there is no such thing as sexual orientation. We are all heterosexual, not homosexual or bisexual. Any deviance from the norm of heterosexuality is *chosen* and is consequently sinful. I have never understood the basis for that argument—biblically, historically, scientifically, or psychologically. There is evidence of human homosexuality across all cultures and across time. In the animal kingdom, penguins, dolphins, bison, swans, giraffes, lions, and chimpanzees have been discovered in same-sex pairings. Nearly 130 bird species have been observed engaging in sexual activities with same-sex partners. More importantly, over the past fifty years, every major medical and psychological organization has acknowledged the existence of sexual orientation and its fixed nature in humans.

It is careless to accuse gays of *choosing* their path of orientation. What is being implied is that they are naturally wired to be straight, but are making the conscious decision to act in direct opposition to this. That would be charging them with the most profound emotional treason.

Using that line of thinking, heterosexuals could be convinced to act in opposition to their "wiring" with enough cajoling, suggestion, support, and prayer. No one wakes up one morning deciding to be heterosexual or homosexual. It is not a *decision* each of us comes to about our orientation, but a *realization*.

Sexual Orientation Does Not Determine Morality

No orientation is inherently moral or immoral. Many Christians portray homosexuals as lustful and promiscuous. They are no more or less so than heterosexuals. It is not one's orientation that causes someone to be faithful or unfaithful, to be honest or to be deceitful, to have a single partner or multiple partners, or to be committed or uncommitted in a relationship. Those decisions or traits are determined by each individual's belief system, not their orientation.

Homosexuality Is Not a Mental Disorder

Much damage has been done to gays and lesbians physically, emotionally, and spiritually because of this harmful classification. The American Medical Association removed homosexuality from its list of mental disorders in 1973. The American Psychiatric Association removed it from the Diagnostic and Statistical Manual of Mental Disorders that year, as well. Since then, every other major medical and psychological association has done so. The American Psychological Association says the following:

> "Lesbian, gay and bisexual orientations are not disorders. Research has found no inherent association between any of these sexual orientations and psychopathology. Both heterosexual behavior and homosexual behavior are normal aspects of human sexuality. Both have been documented in many different cultures and historical eras. Despite the persistence of stereotypes that portray lesbian, gay and bisexual people as disturbed, several decades of research and clinical experience have led all mainstream medical and mental health organizations in this country to conclude that these orientations represent normal forms of human experience. Lesbian, gay and bisexual relationships are normal forms of human bonding. Therefore, these mainstream organizations long ago abandoned classifications of homosexuality as a mental disorder."[1]

Reparative Therapy Does Not Work and Is Damaging

Reparative therapy, by definition, implies that someone must be repaired, that something must be broken. It is based on the assumption that homosexuality is a sin, a mental disorder, and is a choice. Therefore, it can be cured or changed. Another term used, conversion therapy, seeks to "convert" the homosexual to heterosexuality.

Treatments since the late 1890s have included surgical castration, hysterectomies, lobotomies, electric shock, and antipsychotic drugs. Most of these techniques have been outlawed. Talk therapy is the most common therapy today. But some practitioners still use aversion treatments, such as inducing vomiting or paralysis, or having the individual snap an elastic band on his or her wrist when aroused by thoughts or images of the same gender. Others attempt to change thought patterns by reframing desires, redirecting thoughts, or through hypnosis. Hormonal supplements or injections are also employed.

According to a January 2018 UCLA (University of California, Los Angeles) School of Law report, 698,000 adults in the U.S. have received conversion therapy. Fifty percent of that number (350,000) received treatment as adolescents—staggering numbers in light of recent polls, which find a majority of Americans in support of ending the use of conversion therapy.[2] Although under fire and hotly debated, reparative therapy for adults is legal and practiced in all fifty states.

All major national health organizations have officially expressed concerns about therapies promoted to modify sexual orientation.

The American Academy of Pediatrics advises avoidance of any treatment that claims to change a person's sexual orientation, or treatment ideas that see homosexuality as a sickness.[3]

The American Counseling Association opposes the portrayal of lesbian, gay, and bisexual youths and adults as mentally ill due to their sexual orientation, and supports the dissemination of accurate information.[4]

The American Psychiatric Association states that psychotherapeutic modalities to convert or "repair" homosexuality are based on developmental theories whose scientific validity is questionable. Furthermore, anecdotal reports of "cures" are counterbalanced by anecdotal claims of psychological harm. In the last four decades, "reparative" therapists have not produced any rigorous scientific research to substantiate their claims of cure. Until there is such research available, the American Psychiatric Association recommends that ethical practitioners refrain from attempts to change individuals' sexual orientation, keeping in mind the medical dictum to first do no harm.[5]

The American Psychological Association supports the dissemination of accurate information about sexual orientation and mental health, and appropriate interventions in order to counteract bias that is based in ignorance or unfounded beliefs.[6]

The American School Counselor Association establishes that it is not the role of the professional school counselor to attempt to change a student's sexual orientation/gender identity, but instead to provide support to LGBTQ (Lesbian, Gay, Bisexual, Transgender, Questioning) students, to promote student achievement and personal well-being.[7]

The National Association of Social Workers says that sexual orientation conversion therapies assume that homosexual orientation is both pathological and freely chosen. No data demonstrate that reparative or conversion therapies are effective, and, in fact, they may be harmful.[8]

Despite the general consensus of major medical and mental health professions that both heterosexuality and homosexuality are normal expressions of human sexuality, efforts to change sexual orientation through therapy are still adopted by some political and religious organizations. While the Southern Baptist Convention admonishes it as a harmful and ineffective treatment, many others with strongly-held religious beliefs about homosexuality consider reparative therapy to be a "loving and biblical" approach. Legal battles in several states demonstrate the disagreement and controversy over this topic.

As of January 2018, the use of conversion therapy on minors is banned in nine states and the District of Columbia: Vermont, California, New Jersey, Illinois, Oregon, Nevada, New Mexico, Rhode Island, and Connecticut. In December 2015, a jury in New Jersey reached a unanimous verdict, finding a firm that promised to convert young gay men into heterosexuals through conversion therapy violated New Jersey's Consumer Fraud Act.

Five pastors in Illinois filed a lawsuit in April 2016 over the state's conversion therapy ban on gay youth. They argued that clergy should be exempt from a law banning counselors from trying to change a minor's sexual orientation, that it violates their constitutional right to free speech and exercise of religion. The Illinois law states that "no person or entity" may advertise or practice conversion therapy that "represents homosexuality as a mental disease, disorder, or illness."

According to the lawsuit, the pastors argued that "homosexual conduct is contrary to God's purpose for humanity and is a disorder of God's creation, which can be resisted or overcome by those who seek to be faithful to God and His Word."[9] These and other pastors say their young parishioners who have sought counsel have had positive experiences. Similar lawsuits in other states have determined that the conversion therapy ban on youth does not apply to those acting in a pastoral or religious capacity, as long as they do not receive payment.

In all fairness, there are those who have gone through reparative therapy and believe their orientation was changed. It is important to note that those individuals were adults and felt they were not forced into therapy. Their self-reporting should not be denied. Janet Boynes, founder of Janet Boynes Ministries, is the author of *Called Out: A Former Lesbian's Discovery of Freedom*. Boynes chronicled her story of living as a lesbian for fourteen years, until God called her out of the "lifestyle." Some might say she was a bisexual and able to choose heterosexuality. Others would argue that she changed her lesbian "behavior," not her orientation. Regardless, she has the right to believe that her sexual orientation has changed.

However, stories like Janet Boynes's are in the minority. There are so many more gays and lesbians who went through conversion therapy and told stories of being suicidal, humiliated, alienated from their families during therapy, cajoled, bullied, and threatened with expulsion or condemnation. They were defined as sick, sinful, lustful, less than acceptable, and were set up for expectations that they could not meet. Try as they may, they could not change their orientation.

Individual Stories

John Evans cofounded the first ex-gay ministry, Love in Action, in 1973. Years later, Evans left the organization after his best friend, who despaired over his failed attempt to change his orientation, committed suicide. Evans said that most of the people he knew in ex-gay groups were "holding on with white knuckles, trying to be something that they were not."[10] Another former Love in Action director, John Smid, said the "entire ex-gay movement was a sham." He apologized and said he "never met a man who experienced a change from homosexual to heterosexual."[11]

John Paulk wrote about his life as an "ex-ex-gay man" in a 2014 *Politico Magazine* article. For ten years, he was a leading spokesman for reparative therapy and ex-gay ministries. He and his wife, an ex-lesbian, were featured on the cover of *Newsweek* in 1998. They coauthored *Love Won Out: How*

God's Love Helped 2 People Leave Homosexuality and Find Each Other.

"I was in denial. It wasn't in fact true, any of it. Worse than being wrong, it was harmful to many people—and caused me years of pain in my own life...I knew I was living on the inside as two people. I wanted to believe it was true so badly, that not only did I lie to other people, I primarily lied to myself. I wanted my homosexuality to change, but the truth is: For all my public rhetoric, I was never one bit less gay."[12]

Alan Chambers, author of *Leaving Homosexuality* and president of the largest ex-gay ministry, Exodus International, closed the organization in 2013.

"I once led the largest organization in the world dedicated to proclaiming freedom from homosexuality through the power of Jesus Christ. I did so with the best of intentions. I repented publicly. I changed my mind... We are here to reunite with dear friends like Julie, who, in embracing her sexuality, has found peace in the embrace of God."[13]

Christians who support reparative therapy and condemn homosexuality will say that gays and lesbians who do not change their orientation lack faith, don't believe strongly enough, or don't place their trust in God. Rather than reconsider Scriptural interpretation, or become informed about sexual orientation, they continue to demand that homosexuals change their orientation. So many Christian gays and lesbians who have been through reparative therapy had faith, believed, trusted God, and tried their hardest to change their orientation. To continue to demand that of them, even in good faith or intention, is cruel—or, at the very least, lacking in compassion.

Reparative therapy strategies currently used include exorcism, "overdosing on homosexuality" by showing homosexual images then inducing nausea with drugs, hormone injections, reading the Bible, praying, fasting, confessing sin, dating the opposite sex, separation from a smothering mother or distant father, isolation, and encouraging females to wear make-up and dresses—as well as to cook—and males to watch football, participate in male sports, walk and talk masculinely.

> "I was nine years old when I recognized my attractions for the same gender. Praying to God every night and pleading with Him to take my feelings away didn't work. Practically living, eating, and breathing the Bible didn't work. I tried repressing and denying who I was—but nothing changed inside of me. I was taught by my pastors, parents, and peers to hate myself—and *that* worked."

This young man wrote about the torment he experienced growing up as a Christian and gay. It is stories like his that motivated me to write this book.

There is no proof that reparative therapy works, and there is much evidence that it can be harmful. Reparative therapy is premised on a lack of understanding of sexual orientation or the denial of its existence. Advocates for reparative therapy rely on a belief that homosexuality is a sin or mental illness. All of these beliefs or misunderstandings are based on stereotypes of gays and lesbians.

The following chapter will look at twelve commonly held stereotypes, how they developed, and effective ways to critique and address them.

CHAPTER 6

STEREOTYPES AND MYTHS

Stereotyping is as common as the air we breathe. Engaging in critical thinking, being self-aware, and looking at why we believe what we believe about someone different from ourselves are all essential to countering stereotypes. The goal is to prevent stereotypes in the first place, or, at the very least, question and understand how they develop. It is also important to understand the damaging effects of stereotypes and the negative impact they have on those who are targeted.

Bad Marriages Lead to Lesbianism

"My wife knows two different women that turned gay after their marriages went bad."

I open the chapter with this stereotype and quote because it is more lighthearted and not as damaging as other stereotypes or myths. Most would smile at the assumption that a bad marriage could cause a woman to become a lesbian. The previous chapter discussed how sexual orientation cannot be changed. The two women in this quote could have been bisexuals, or women who later realized they were lesbians.

Half of heterosexual marriages end in divorce. That would mean that a majority of divorced females could potentially be lesbians. According to a 2017 Gallup Poll, 4.4% of women in the United States identify themselves as lesbians.[1] Because polls cannot take into account those who are closeted, some estimate the numbers to be at 5 to 10%. Others say that number is too high and falsely drawn from the sex researcher Alfred Kinsey's 1960s reports. All would agree, however, that a majority of divorced women are not lesbians.

Homosexuality Is a Sinful Lifestyle

"There is a difference between someone who committed a sin and someone who sins as a lifestyle. That's the difference between a sheep in the mud and a pig in the mud."

"I do not hate gay people. I am against their lifestyle. I do not believe in the homosexual lifestyle."

Two words to consider in this myth: "sinful" and "lifestyle." Chapter 4 addressed the Scriptures used to condemn homosexuality as a sin. Chapter 5 discussed sexual orientation. Interpretation of those Scriptures and belief of what constitutes orientation determine if someone considers homosexuality a sin.

I do not interpret the Scriptures to be condemning of homosexuals as sinful. There is no evidence (emotionally, spiritually, relationally) to indicate that I am living in sin—or anyone else is in sin based upon their sexual orientation. It is someone's interpretation over mine. I do not judge anyone else's life, their sinfulness, or make any accusations or edicts. At the very least, we should leave that to God and not make sweeping judgments to determine who is sinning. We should not rank-order sin by placing homosexuality at the top of the list. As for "lifestyle," there is no such thing as a "heterosexual lifestyle" any more than there is a homosexual lifestyle. These terms have no real meaning or value. They speak no truth about any of us and serve no purpose other than to demean or avoid respectful dialogue.

Gays and Lesbians Are Promiscuous

Because homosexuality is so often inaccurately defined in terms of sex acts, homosexuals are overidentified with sex. This has led to a belief that they are promiscuous, and that homosexuality naturally leads to promiscuity.

Christians who consider homosexuals to be sinners take it one step further by citing Romans 1:24–32 (NKJV), to claim that God "gave them up to uncleanness, in the lusts of their hearts, to dishonor their bodies among themselves." The conclusion then is that those who are openly gay are inviting sin into their lives and giving themselves up to promiscuity.

As was discussed in Chapter 4, Paul described in his letter to the Romans what happened to followers of Christ who turned to idols and to other religions. He specifically addressed Roman fertility cults, where men and women engaged in sexual orgies. He emphasized that rebellion against God has consequences. Paul followed with a lengthy list of other activities and attitudes as wicked among the rebellious. Too often, these verses have been used solely to decry homosexuals and to justify perpetuating the myth that gays and lesbians are wanton.

Claims that gay men have a high number of sexual partners can be traced to 1970s studies. In the midst of the "sexual revolution," subjects in those studies were recruited from gay bars, bathhouses, and other situations organized around sexual activity. Similarly, high numbers of sexual partners have been reported among heterosexual males at that time. It is not about homosexuality or sexual orientation, but perhaps the social conditioning or acceptance around sexual activity for males, gay or straight. No such reports exist regarding lesbians having a higher number of sexual partners than heterosexual women.

Gay Men Are Child Molesters

Child molesting, or pedophilia, has nothing to do with sexual orientation. Paraphilia is a medical term that refers to a class of sexual disorders recognized by the American Psychiatric Association. Pedophilia is one of a number of sexual disorders grouped together with paraphilia. Other examples of paraphilia are fetishism, masochism, exhibitionism, and voyeurism. Paraphilic disorders are sexual, ongoing, and can be diagnosed.

Pedophilia is not a mystery and experts claim that 95% of child molestation can be prevented.[2] But one of the greatest obstacles is people's fear of the facts about child molestation. Misinformation has led to widespread silence and protection of the abuser, as well as a prevailing false belief that homosexual men constitute the majority of molesters. This could not be further from the truth.

According to the Child Molestation Research & Prevention Institute, an estimated one in twenty teenage boys and adult men sexually abuse children, and an estimated one teenage girl or adult woman in every 3,300 molests children. Of the over 16,000 people in the original sample in the Child Molestation Prevention Study, only 601 abusers were women. Of the 4000 people who admitted to being a child molester, only 1.4%, or 55, of them were women.[3]

So who is the *typical* child molester according to these studies? Researchers asked the 4,000 admitted child molesters in the Abel and Harlow Child Molestation Prevention Study to answer questions about their lives. These abusers were men aged eighteen to eighty; 77% were married or formerly married. More than 46% had some college education and another 30% were high school graduates; 65% were working. Numerous studies of adult victims have sought to link child-molestation victims to lower social class and lower family income. All have failed. Child victims and abusers exist equally in families of all income levels and classes. In the study, 93% of molesters were identified as religious. Child molesters are statistically heterosexual males, married, educated, employed, and as religious as any other American male.[4]

Children are most at risk from the adults in their own family, and from the adults who are in their parents' social circle. In fact, 90% of abusers target children in their own families, as well as children they know well.[5] Research suggests that the risk is across the board: Child molesters come from every part of our society. Sadly, children from every part of our society are at risk. The majority of molesters are heterosexual males. There is no link to homosexuality or sexual orientation.

Homosexuals Are Emotionally Unhealthy

"Members of the non-heterosexual population are estimated to have about 1.5 times higher risk of experiencing anxiety disorders than members of the heterosexual population, as well as roughly double the risk of depression, 1.5 times the risk of substance abuse, and nearly 2.5 times the risk of suicide."[6]

—THE NEW ATLANTIS SPECIAL REPORT

Conservative and liberal research foundations report similar statistics regarding anxiety, depression, substance abuse, and suicide. It is tragic that homosexuals are represented at a higher level and are generally more at risk than heterosexuals. Granted, lesbians and gays suffer emotional distress from social oppression and opposition. They are labeled as sinners, accused of going to Hell, shunned or forced out of Churches, excluded or ignored within their own families, and can still be denied services in some establishments.

My last chapter will explore what can be done to reduce the negative and harmful impact on gays and lesbians emotionally, physically, and spiritually. Are all homosexuals, or even a majority of them, emotionally unhealthy? Of course not. Can the rate of depression, anxiety, substance abuse, and suicide among gays be correlated to the degree of their exposure to hostility, rejection, demands to change sexual orientation, and claims that they are bound for Hell? Logically and anecdotally, yes, but no research has been conducted that separates the numbers by religious affiliation, familial relationships, and identified levels of social oppression.

Regardless of whether or not the correlation has been researched or proven, it is far different from assuming that the cause of distress and any emotional unhealthiness is sexual orientation itself. It is the hateful and negative behaviors and attitudes imposed on gays *because* of their sexual orientation by families, Churches, and society.

Homosexuals Cannot Sustain Long-Term Relationships

The divorce rate among heterosexuals is purportedly at fifty percent, but there is no agreement as to the exact percentages. Since gays and lesbians were not legally allowed to marry until June 2015, long-term statistical data cannot be derived. There is no evidence to suggest that someone's sexual orientation determines the length of a relationship.

However, lack of support or recognition for gay relationships can affect the length of time gay couples remain together. There are many examples of homosexuals who have been together for twenty, thirty, or forty years, even in the midst of discrimination and negative reaction from families and society. In fact, the woman to whom I dedicated this book was in a fifty-one-year relationship with her female partner. Marriage takes commitment and work. Outside negative forces aimed at couples can add to the likelihood of strife or dissolution of a marriage, regardless of sexual orientation itself.

Homosexuality Is Demonic and a Curse

This myth is rooted in the interpretation of Scriptures as condemning of homosexuality. That if it is sin, it is not of God. If it is not of God, the conclusion for some Christians is that it is demonic or of the Devil. There are gay and lesbian Christians who have submitted themselves to exorcism in the hopes of curing their homosexuality. There may be a few who claim they were freed of the "demon of homosexuality." As with reparative therapy, it is not my right to deny someone else's experiences and claims. I will speak for those I personally know who had exorcism thrust upon them, were humiliated, and were forced to either accept "demonic delivery" or leave the Church.

It is hard to see how love, mutuality, and commitment in homosexual relationships can be demonic. Even if homosexuals are involved in uncommitted, non-monogamous relationships, as are many heterosexuals, why would anyone take it upon themselves to judge, to determine it as demonic, and to demand deliverance? If it is the belief system of all involved, that is their business, as long as no one is coerced, shamed, or given ultimatums to undergo deliverance. That would only amount to cruelty in the name of Christ.

Homosexuality Can Be Compared to Alcoholism

"I had the temptation to indulge in alcohol and drugs just like gays. I have overcome those temptations."

"I may have the genetic coding that I'm inclined to be an alcoholic, but I have the desire not to do that, and I look at the homosexual issue the same way."[7]

—RICK PERRY, FORMER TEXAS GOVERNOR

Comparing alcohol and drug abuse to homosexuality is nothing new. That comparison relies on the belief that homosexuality is a disorder or mental illness. The American Medical Association (AMA) and the American Psychiatric Association (APA) debunked that claim in the 1970s. However, alcoholism remains on the DSM (Diagnostic and Statistical Manual of Mental Disorders) list, with the AMA defining it as "an addiction to the consumption of alcoholic liquor or the mental illness and compulsive behavior resulting from alcohol dependency."

Alcohol and drugs are substances. Homosexuals are humans with relationships that involve affection, physical attraction, intimacy, and sexual expression.

These two quotes also assume that homosexuality is a choice and equate it to choosing to drink alcohol. There is no proof that sexual orientation is a choice. As discussed in the previous chapter, sexual *behavior* is a choice, not sexual orientation.

Alcoholism has many negative consequences. It is what one does or how one behaves within his or her sexual orientation that determines negative or positive consequences, not the orientation itself. According to the APA:

"Alcohol abuse is a drinking pattern that results in significant and recurrent adverse consequences. Alcohol abusers may fail to fulfill major school, work, or family obligations... Although severe alcohol problems get the most public attention, even mild to moderate problems cause substantial damage to individuals, their families, and their communities."[8]

Alcoholism is a disorder. Homosexuality is a sexual orientation.

Homosexuality Is Unnatural

"It's just a decision. I don't support the choice to be unnatural. Just be straight like the rest of us."

—Anonymous

"I do believe that being homosexual is NOT NATURAL. I say this because of the obvious. Men and women are different and have different reproductive organs for that very reason, to procreate. I do not believe God means for people of the same sex to be together. It's against the normal order of things and certainly not God's will for procreation."

—Anonymous

"It seems like to me, a vagina—as a man—would be more desirable than a man's anus. That's just me. I'm just thinking: There's more there! She's got more to offer. I mean, come on, dudes! You know what I'm saying? But hey, sin: it's not logical, my man. It's just not logical."[9]

—Phil Robertson, December 2013

All three of these comments are from heterosexuals. For *them*, homosexuality is not natural, not relatable, not understandable. They are speaking from their own hetero-sexual perspective and experience, which they have every right to do. But each of these statements takes it one step further—a request for gays to be straight like themselves, a determination that sex is only for those who procreate, and judgment that all things homosexual are undesirable and unnatural. Many heterosexuals hold this belief. It is unfortunate that something someone disagrees with, doesn't understand, or can't relate to is then deemed unnatural for all others. Because homosexuality is not "natural" to many heterosexuals, it does not make it unnatural by default. None of us can agree, or needs to agree, on what is natural or desirable in the privacy of someone else's bedroom or sexual expression.

As for natural versus unnatural—interracial marriage, race-mixing, marriage without procreation, women wearing pants, women voting or running for political office—have all been deemed unnatural at one time or another.

Gays Recruit

"As a mother, I know that homosexuals cannot biologically reproduce children; therefore, they must recruit our children."[10]

—Anita Bryant, 1977

This myth relies on the belief that someone can be convinced to change his or her sexual orientation from heterosexual to homosexual. That may be the *fear*, but again, there is no basis or proof that sexual orientation can be changed. Sexual behavior, maybe, but why would someone who is not bisexual or homosexual be susceptible to so-called recruitment if they are heterosexual?

To the contrary, if gays *could* recruit, then heterosexuals could also. That, ironically, is the basis for reparative therapy—heterosexual recruitment or therapy. Again, there is no proof of the effectiveness of reparative therapy. There are countless testimonies against it and to the subsequent damage invoked.

If by "recruitment" one is referring to molestation, no one should be forced or taken advantage of sexually, children or adults. Whatever the orientation, such abuse is wrong, and can cause long-lasting emotional harm. But there is no evidence that it changes the victim's sexual orientation.

There Is a Homosexual Agenda

"The truth is that the objective of the homosexual campaign is not about American freedom. The objective is the delegitimization and annihilation of Christianity in America."[11]

—Star Parker, April 2015

This statement stokes the flames of fear among Christian heterosexuals. It assumes that there is a monolithic gay population. Neither gays nor heterosexuals *all* believe the same, nor *all* have the same attitude, nor *all* have the same focus or purpose in life. To claim otherwise is incendiary, sensational, and simply untrue.

A "homosexual agenda" implies that gays recruit, are out to destroy Christianity, and are plotting to take over the American economy and society. Gays cannot recruit any more than heterosexuals can. Christianity is not at risk of being annihilated, with Christians accounting for 72% of the population, and a 5 to 10% gay population is not large enough to dominate politically or economically.

Homosexuality Threatens Family Values

"[Homosexuality] is Satan's diabolical attack upon the family, a symptom of a sin-sick society that will not only have a corrupting influence upon our next generation, but it will also bring down the wrath of God upon America."[12]

—JERRY FALWELL

Pitting homosexuality against family values is not new. If American families are under siege from homosexuals, where is the direct correlation? How do gays impact, attack, or destroy heterosexual families? Is the implication that, given the opportunity, many heterosexuals would flock to homosexuality, that heterosexual families would disappear for lack of interest? Of course not.

I do not mock Christian concerns over the breakdown in the stability and integrity of the family. The "standard" nuclear family—with two parents married for life—is now the exception, not the rule. But homosexuality is not the cause of these social changes. Further discussion about those changes would be the topic of another book.

Family values are about loyalty, love, trust, and putting the family first. The term "pro-family" has often been used exclusively in reference to Christians and heterosexuals. Non-Christians and homosexuals can also be pro-family. They, too, can and do embrace such ideals as love, loyalty, trust, and putting family first.

Claims that gays threaten family values, have an agenda, recruit, are promiscuous, or are child molesters are all stereotypes that polarize and demonize gays and lesbians. They are broad and false generalizations that are damaging to millions.

The ensuing chapter will demonstrate how these stereotypes and myths have been popularized and perpetuated by ministers and Church doctrines over time. Without questioning or criticizing the use of stereotypes, they will remain powerful and damaging. We will hear from well-known ministers and the Churches they represent in the following chapter.

CHAPTER 7

MINISTERS AND CHURCHES

Religious reasons have been cited throughout our history in building a case for homosexuals as sinners, deviants, mentally ill, anti-God, and in need of change or redemption. Ministers often preach this from their pulpits. Christian church denominations have spoken out against homosexuality and have put written policy in place. Understandably, ministers speak to the like-minded. They are respected and address their congregations without challenge or disagreement on their beliefs about homosexuals. Most often, followers or adherents already have similar beliefs, or they develop their beliefs based upon what they hear from trusted leaders.

This process makes sense. There is no inherent harm if congregants choose ministers whose sermons match their beliefs. The harm can be in the sway that ministers and evangelists hold as religious leaders. They have every right to speak out, to speak of their convictions, and to speak to their base. But in so doing, they should consider the impact of the words they use and the sentiments behind their beliefs and claims about homosexuals.

The following quotes speak for themselves. These are well-respected ministers, evangelists, and heads of ministries who have had a positive impact on many lives. The previous chapter addressed myths and stereotypes, and traced their development. This chapter will show how stereotypes are often reinforced or perpetuated by those in the pulpit and the Churches they represent.

Jerry Falwell

"Homosexuals are brute beasts...part of a vile and satanic system that will be utterly annihilated and there will be a celebration in heaven."[1]

Founder of Liberty University, evangelist Jerry Falwell was respected by many Christians. He was influential in leading the Moral Majority crusade in the 1980s. The words used in this quote are particularly extreme and damaging to homosexuals.

Pat Robertson

"If the world accepts homosexuality as its norm and if it moves the entire world in that regard, the whole world is then going to be sitting like Sodom and Gomorrah before a Holy God."[2]

"From a biblical standpoint, the rise of homosexuality is a sign that a society is in the last stages of decay."[3]

There is no evidence that homosexuality is on the rise in the United States or any other country. There is disagreement as to what percent of our population is homosexual. Researchers maintain that the percentage of homosexuals and heterosexuals throughout human history has remained fairly static.

The widespread acceptance of "same-sex behavior" among the ancient Greeks has been cited as an example of increased numbers of homosexuals leading to the fall of an empire. Greek males engaging in sex with male adults and boys was more about status and patriarchy than homosexual orientation. There is no direct link between homosexuality and the Greeks being overtaken by the Romans.

Sex researcher Alfred Kinsey estimated that the number of homosexuals in the U.S. ranged between 4 and 15%. Dr. Paul Gebhart of the Institute for Sex Research claimed to have used newer statistical methods to arrive at approximately 9.3%.[4] Self-reporting is not accurate since so many homosexuals still remain closeted. Many over the years have felt pressured or were uncertain about the safety of revealing their same-sex orientation to researchers.

There may *appear* to be a rise in homosexuality as more gays and lesbians are "out" in their private and work lives, are participating in marches and demonstrations, and are more active in political arenas. As gays and lesbians feel more legally protected from workplace or personal discrimination, they have become more vocal and visible. There has also been an increase in representation of gays in the movies and on television.

Televangelist Pat Robertson founded the Christian Broadcasting Network (CBN) and still appears on his television show *The 700 Club*. He has remained consistent in preaching against the sin of homosexuality, and that it will lead to the downfall of America.

Anita Bryant

"What these people (homosexuals) really want, hidden behind obscure legal phrases, is the legal right to propose to our children that theirs is an acceptable alternate way of life... I will lead such a crusade to stop it as this country has not seen before."[5]

In the 1970s, Anita Bryant was the public leader for Save Our Children, a political coalition that was against homosexuality, and sought to overturn an ordinance that prohibited discrimination in housing, employment, and public accommodation. She later formed Anita Bryant Ministries International and still runs the organization today.

She was lauded by many Christians for standing by "her biblical convictions and what the Bible said." One Christian commentator said, "Seldom in twentieth-century history has one person been subjected to the kind of attack Anita Bryant endured."

Anita wrote in her book, *At Any Cost* (1978), that protest marches and demonstrations involving hundreds of thousands were staged from coast to coast. She was the butt of jokes on radio and TV. She and her family received death threats, prank phone calls, bomb scares, and hate mail. There was a groundswell of support for her from Christians, but she felt that, for the most part, "the media chose to support the homosexual community." The animosity from the gay community culminated in the infamous pie-in-the-face debacle.

Anita Bryant did become a target. It is unfortunate that she and her family were threatened. Having a pie thrown in her face at a public event was embarrassing. Humiliation, death threats, and nasty jokes should never be condoned. Anita incurred the wrath of many homosexuals, who felt that *they* were directly targeted by her and her campaign against homosexuality. Gays have often experienced humiliation, death threats, or been the butt of nasty jokes. No one deserves that kind of treatment—Anita Bryant or homosexuals. It is unfortunate that Ms. Bryant characterized gays as evil, sinful, perverted, molesters, and recruiters. All are stereotypes that no one would want to be on the receiving end of—all are polarizing labels. Labels that harm, that dehumanize, and point to a group of people as less than. It is a case in point as to why we need to move away from the damaging "us versus them" rhetoric and behavior.

Anne Graham Lotz

"America is imploding morally and spiritually. God is removing His blessing and protection from us, leaving us to our sins. That encroaching judgment is evident in the chaos of the political scene, the economy, and even the weather (in reference to homosexuality and other sins)."

"Romans 1 describes the type of judgment where we sin, and we refuse to repent of our sin, then He backs away from us. He removes Himself from us and He turns us over to ourselves. That's what I see in America. I believe we're entering into that phase of judgment, where God is backing away."

"There is a sense that America is unraveling."[6]

Daughter of evangelist Billy Graham and sister to Franklin Graham, Anne Graham Lotz is a religious leader in her own right. She founded AnGel Ministries, holds six honorary degrees, and has authored eleven books. She includes homosexuality in a list of sins that are taking down the country.

Franklin Graham

"Putin was right on how the Russian government dealt with its LGBT activists. Obviously, he may be wrong about many things, but he has taken a stand to protect his nation's children from the damaging effects of any gay and lesbian agenda."[7]

"The Girl Scouts organization sure isn't what it used to be! St. Louis Archbishop Robert Carlson isn't worried about being politically correct in letting people know about it either. He told church members and scout leaders that the Girl Scouts is wrong in their support of transgender rights and homosexuality and is not aligned with the teachings of his church. I don't know about you, but I won't be buying any Girl Scout cookies this year."[8]

"To change my view that homosexual behavior is sinful would require God to change His word on the topic and God doesn't change. His Word is the same yesterday and today, and a million years from now. But to wink at sin and to tell somebody it's okay, when I know the consequence of what will happen one day when they have to stand before God. So I want to warn people, and I think the Pope is right when he says he is not the judge. God is the judge."[9]

"If they (homosexuals) choose to continue to live in sin, God is going to judge them one day and they'll be separated from Him for eternity in hell."

"Well, I've never really been one to try to be politically correct. I just feel truth is truth, and sometimes I probably offend some people."

"Gay couples can recruit. You can adopt a child into a marriage, but you can also recruit children into your cause. I believe in protecting children from exploitation—all exploitation."[10]

Graham suggested that his blunt remarks about LGBT activists and those "living in sin" were rooted in tough love. He asserted that gay couples who want to adopt children are possibly looking to indoctrinate them with a "pernicious" worldview. Of course, ALL children should be protected from exploitation—sexually, physically, emotionally. However, he is playing on stereotypes that gays recruit, molest, are promiscuous, and have an agenda.

Franklin Graham oversees the Billy Graham Evangelistic Association and the international Christian relief group, Samaritan's Purse. He is a well-respected author and evangelist. I admire much of his work but disagree with his beliefs about homosexuality.

Phil Robertson

"STDs are spread as God's punishment for sexual immorality. Do you think it's a coincidence that all of these debilitating—and literally that can cause death—diseases follow that kind of conduct? God says, one woman, one man, and everyone says, oh that's old hat, that's that old Bible stuff. But I'm thinking…a disease-free guy and a disease-free woman, they marry and they keep their sex between the two of them. They're not going to get chlamydia, and gonorrhea, and syphilis, and AIDS (acquired immunodeficiency syndrome). It's safe."[11]

Yes, it is safe to be disease-free, monogamous, or to have protected sex in any relationship. Chlamydia, gonorrhea, syphilis, and AIDS are no respecter of persons. Heterosexuals, bisexuals, homosexuals, male and female can contract these diseases if they participate in unsafe or unprotected sexual activity.

Since the 1990s AIDS epidemic, some ministers have preached that AIDS was God's punishment for homosexuality. That statement is lacking in both compassion and fact. Heterosexuals are now most affected by AIDS worldwide. And, if God was punishing homosexuality, it impacted half of the homosexual population: gay men. By that rationale, lesbians were left unpunished with very few documented cases.

Lesser-Known Ministers

"Homosexuality is a terrible thing. It's an abomination, so we are trying to inform people on exactly what Scripture says about it. Homosexuals are destroying this society."

A Georgia minister said he would die before accepting gay members into his congregation.

"Homosexuals are perverts and predators."

A Sacramento, California, minister preached this from the pulpit while citing Judges 19, Genesis 4, and Romans 1.

"We the People are tired of having a radical agenda forced upon our families. We the People are tired of the bullying and the harassment. We the People are tired of being marginalized."

A Protestant minister in Houston responded to the defeat of an LGBT nondiscrimination ordinance. He and others were relieved and felt that their beliefs and way of life had been under attack by gay activists.

"Liberals haven't abandoned the concept of sin, but the definition of sin has changed. It used to be that homosexual acts were considered sinful, but today criticism of homosexual acts is considered sinful."

A Florida minister said the definition of sin has changed in regard to homosexuality. I say it is the *interpretation* of the Scriptures that have been used to condemn homosexuals that has changed. Criticizing homosexual acts in and of itself is not sinful. Denigrating and denying gays and lesbians the right to marry, to be in a relationship, to participate in Churches, or to be accepted within their families could be considered sinful.

Billboards

"Homosexuality Is a Death Worthy Crime! Leviticus 20:13"

"Gay and Lesbians Are Disgraces to Humanity! Leviticus 20:13"

A minister defended these signs that stood in front of his church in Georgia, declaring that it was his job to teach people about evil. He said he didn't condone violence against the gay community, but called for a judicial statute condemning homosexuality.

"Homosexuality Is a Behavior, Not a Civil Right"

A billboard purchased by a church group was placed on a heavily trafficked street in Michigan. Homosexuality is a sexual orientation, and, it IS a civil right.

Churches Requiring Repentance and Change

Little wonder there is a strong bias and negative sentiment that so many Christians hold toward gays and lesbians if they attend Churches that preach homosexuality as sinful and an abomination. I've asked many members of these Churches why they believe that homosexuals are going to Hell. Most cannot cite the exact Scriptures but are sure there are many throughout the Bible. Sodom and Gomorrah are often referenced, and some recall something about men not laying with men. They have always believed that homosexuality was wrong, family and friends said so, and trusted ministers of their Churches preached it. These Christians are well-meaning and often emphasize hating the sin, but loving the sinner. They believe that all homosexuals need to repent and change. If Church doctrine states it, and the Bible says so, it must be so.

I am not mocking these Churches and their members. I am challenging those who believe homosexuality is a sin to familiarize themselves with their Church doctrine. Read the Scriptures for themselves, preferably read Chapter 4 in my book, and draw their own conclusions. Doctrine from the Southern Baptist, Jehovah's Witnesses, Mormon and Catholic Churches are detailed below. There are many faithful adherents, and based on Church doctrine, most would argue that homosexuality is abhorrent and gays and lesbians are going to Hell without repentance and change. These are only four of many Churches and denominations that hold these beliefs.

Southern Baptist Convention (SBC)

"We affirm God's plan for marriage and sexual intimacy—one man, and one woman, for life. Homosexuality is not a valid alternative lifestyle. The Bible condemns it as sin. It is not, however, unforgivable sin. The same redemption available to all sinners is available to homosexuals. They, too, may become new creations in Christ.[12]

—SBC WEB SITE, 2017

This statement declares homosexuality to be a sin and refers to it as an invalid alternative lifestyle. As a sin and a "lifestyle," not a sexual orientation, it is forgivable. Grace and acceptance are offered, and members can be redeemed, *if* they change to heterosexuality or remain celibate.

Jehovah's Witnesses

"Although the Bible condemns homosexual acts, it does not encourage prejudice, hate crimes, or any other kind of mistreatment of homosexuals… Romans 12:18"

"The Bible dignifies humans by assuring them that they can choose not to act on their improper sexual urges… Colossians 3:15"[13]

—*THE WATCHTOWER* AND *AWAKE!* 2016

It is good that prejudice and mistreatment of homosexuals are not encouraged. Most other denominations either explicitly or implicitly state the same. However, if members do not repent, change their orientation, or remain celibate, they will be disfellowshipped. Fellow members are required to shun them completely, avoiding all contact.

While the above 2016 quote expresses a balanced and tolerant view, homosexuality in the past has been described by *The Watchtower* as: abhorrent, sexually degrading, unnatural sexual perversion, disgraceful sexual appetites, obscene, detestable, and repulsive.

Mormon Church

"If you decide to share your experiences of feeling same-sex attraction or to openly identify as gay, you should be supported and treated with kindness and respect, both at home and in church. We all need to be patient with each other as we figure things out."

—LDS.ORG, 2017-08-21

This statement is kindly and compassionately written. However, "as we figure things out" means going back to the Scriptures as interpreted by the Church. One must be celibate or change to heterosexuality in order to remain in good standing with the Latter-Day Saints (LDS).

"Sexual relations are proper only between a man and a woman who are legally and lawfully wedded as husband and wife. Any other sexual relations, including those between persons of the same gender, are sinful and undermine the divinely created institution of the family. The Church accordingly affirms defining marriage as the legal and lawful union between a man and a woman."

—*HANDBOOK 2: ADMINISTERING THE CHURCH*,
APRIL 21, 2010

The LDS Church recognizes that feelings of same-sex attraction may not change or be overcome. They expect unmarried members, gay or straight, to abstain from any and all sexual relations outside of marriage. Their definition of marriage as only between a man and a woman leaves no room for homosexuals in a monogamous, committed relationship. The following chapter will look at all aspects of the arguments for and against gay/same-sex marriage.

Roman Catholic Church

"The Church seeks to enable every person to live out the universal call to holiness. Persons with a homosexual inclination ought to receive every aid and encouragement to embrace this call personally and fully. This will unavoidably involve much struggle and self-mastery, for following Jesus always means following the way of the Cross."

—*MINISTRY TO PERSONS WITH A HOMOSEXUAL INCLINATION*, USCCB (2006)

"Basing itself on Sacred Scripture, which presents homosexual acts as acts of grave depravity, tradition has always declared that homosexual acts are intrinsically disordered." (2357)

"The number of men and women who have deep-seated homosexual tendencies is not negligible. This inclination, which is objectively disordered, constitutes for most of them a trial. They must be accepted with respect, compassion, and sensitivity." (2358)

"Homosexual persons are called to chastity." (2359)

—*CATECHISM OF THE CATHOLIC CHURCH*, ARTICLE 6

These are compassionately written statements from the U.S. Conference of Catholic Bishops and the *Catechism of the Catholic Church*, but with requirements to abstain from sexual activity. Homosexuality as an *orientation* is not technically considered sinful by the Catholic Church, though it is referred to as an "objective disorder." The Church recognizes that it is an innate condition in most cases, not a choice, and therefore cannot be considered a sin. Homosexual *sexual activity*, however, is seen as a moral disorder, against natural law, and sinful.

Each of the four Churches mentioned distinguish between inclination, attraction, tendency, or orientation AND homosexual relationships, lifestyles, practices, or sexual activity. With that distinction comes acceptance and compassion for the person and the so-called "condition" of homosexuality, but not for the actions or involvement sexually, emotionally, or spiritually between two men or two women. Good standing within these Churches is dependent upon repentance, celibacy, or change to heterosexuality.

Churches that Believe Homosexuality Is Not a Sin

Some may view this section of the chapter as a liberal versus conservative issue among Churches and denominations. It is easy to single-handedly dismiss a church's belief or stance by writing them off as liberal or conservative. In an attempt to not reinforce this *us versus them* mentality, I ask readers to consider viewpoints expressed by Churches and ministers with whom they might disagree. The following statements are compassionate, well-thought, based on Scriptures, and provide much-needed healing.[14]

Baptist – Dr. Stayton

"There is nothing in the Bible, or in my own theology, that would lead me to believe that God regards homosexuality as sin. God is interested in our relationships with ourselves, others, the things in our lives, and with God (Matthew 23:36–40). There is nothing in the mind of God that could be against a loving, sexual relationship, freely entered into, without coercion, among sincere adults, whether gay, bisexual, or straight."

Lutheran – Bishop Olson

"God could not care less about humanly devised categories that label and demean those who somehow do not fit into the norm of those in control… How we live our lives in either affirming or destructive ways is God's concern, but being either homosexually oriented or heterosexually oriented is neither a divine plus or minus."

Judaism – Rabbi Lazar

"First of all, I do not know what God thinks. In my opinion, homosexuality is not a sin, but an alternate lifestyle. In my opinion, homosexuality by itself is not immoral. When sex is used to corrupt, for prurient and/or exploitative purposes or selfish reasons or to hurt someone else, this is immoral."

Presbyterian – Dr. Edwards

"God does not regard homosexuality as a sin any more than heterosexuality. Sin is lack of respect or love for God. It is a lack of love or respect for other persons."

Roman Catholic – Sister Ford

"Two truths are especially relevant in thinking this through. First we have a theological point. God, the one who has made all of creation, loves and cherishes all creatures without exception. Second, modern psychology shows us that homosexual orientation is set by age five or six. Most psychologists agree that it is not a matter of choice, whether orientation is inborn as some think, or acquired very early, as others say. How then could an all-loving God possibly violate Divine nature and regard homosexuals as 'sinners?'"

Episcopal – Bishop Spong

"There is nothing unnatural about any shared love, even between two of the same gender, if that experience calls both partners into a fuller state of being. Contemporary research is uncovering new facts that are producing a rising conviction that homosexuality, far from being a sickness, sin, perversion or unnatural act, is a healthy, natural, and affirming form of human sexuality for some people. Findings indicate that homosexuality is a given fact in the nature of a significant portion of people, and that it is unchangeable."

United Church of Christ – Dr. Nelson

"I am convinced that our sexuality and our sexual orientations, whatever they may be, are a gift from God. Sexual sin does not reside in our orientations, but rather in expressing our sexuality in ways that harm, oppress, or use others for our own selfish gratification. When we express ourselves sexually in ways that are loving and just, faithful and responsible, then I am convinced that God celebrates our sexuality, whatever our orientation may be."

This chapter covered an array of religious beliefs with regard to homosexuality. Many ministers and Churches declare it to be a sin and demand repentance, celibacy, and change from homosexuals. In the course of preaching heartfelt and Scriptural beliefs, some ministers have villainized homosexuality and have perpetuated myths and stereotypes about homosexuals. Or, at the very least, broad, hurtful generalizations have gone unchallenged.

The disagreement and debate among denominations over homosexuality has led to a polarizing of beliefs and stances—for and against gay marriage.

The subsequent chapter will take a closer look at these arguments and the impact they have on gays and lesbians, in our Churches, and throughout our society.

CHAPTER 8

Marriage

Religious Beliefs vs Right to Marry

There are two distinct sides to the marriage issue: those who oppose homosexuality, consider it sinful, and believe that homosexuals are condemned to Hell, and those who believe that it is a civil right to choose who to marry, that the government should not deny the right to marry based on sexual orientation, and that gays and lesbians should be included in the definition of marriage. The debate has heated since the 2015 Supreme Court decision overturned state laws that denied gay couples the right to marry.

It would stand to reason that anyone who believes God and the Scriptures condemn homosexuality would also oppose same-sex marriage. The question is how to negotiate religious beliefs that are in opposition to a group of citizens marrying when the Supreme Court has determined it unconstitutional to deny that group the right. Which should win out? Religious institutions, state laws, federal laws, Supreme Court decisions?

In this chapter, I will uncover the nuances of the debates for and against gay marriage. Some may say it is now the law of the land and there is no reason to debate it. Others hear the heated rhetoric and are puzzled as to how to bridge the gap between opposing sides. Yet others have challenged same-sex marriage, are determined to change state and federal laws, pass amendments, or overturn the 2015 Supreme Court decision. All are avenues or options in a democracy where citizens of all beliefs can exercise their rights and expect to be heard.

While both sides of this debate remain firmly planted in their stances, the arguments have spread into everyday life: clerks of court denying marriage licenses, ministers and religious groups issuing statements that they will only honor marriages between a man and a woman, bakeries and florists refusing services based on their religious beliefs. A recent Facebook post characterized this developing *us vs them* position:

"I am sick and tired of seeing: Christianity Smeared, Traditional Marriage Destroyed, Good People Mocked for Believing in Jesus Christ."

Many Christians feel under attack by what they consider liberal legislation and a redefining of marriage. Gays and lesbians feel under attack by religious groups who want to dismantle laws allowing them to marry, and who insist that marriage should be reserved for heterosexual males and females.

How do we honor the rights of each of these groups without denying the rights of the other? I will attempt to answer that question in the following chapters. First, it is important to look at how marriage has been defined throughout U.S. history, the purposes of marriage, what restrictions or requirements have been placed on marriage in the past, and who has the right to define marriage.

Definitions of Marriage

Courts have upheld or reversed laws regarding marriage and marriage equality over the years. Justices often turn to dictionaries for clarification, interpretation, and confirmation. The dictionary definition of marriage remained constant as between one male and one female until recently. That history or tradition is cited by conservatives as the basis for maintaining the definition.

In Samuel Johnson's *A Dictionary of the English Language* (1755), the definition is simply stated as "the act of uniting a man and a woman for life."

Noah Webster included civil and religious purposes of marriage in the *An American Dictionary of the English Language* (1828): "the act of uniting a man and woman for life; wedlock: the legal union of a man and woman for life. Marriage is a contract both civil and religious, by which the parties engage to live together in mutual affection and fidelity, till death shall separate them. Marriage was instituted by God himself for the purpose of preventing the promiscuous intercourse of the sexes, for promoting domestic felicity, and for securing the maintenance and education of children."

The Century Dictionary and Cyclopedia (1891) was the first dictionary to be based on scientific and linguistic principles. It stresses the civil nature of marriage. It is also the first dictionary to recognize that marriage is defined differently in different cultures: "Marriage may include both common law marriage and 'plural marriage,' or *polygamy* (not just abroad but even in the United States as practiced by Mormons). Also "marriage is an engagement entered into by mutual consent, and has for its end the propagation of the species."

Black's Law Dictionary (2nd edition, 1910) restates earlier definitions that specify heterosexual monogamy, but it grounds the institution of marriage in civil law rather than religion: "Marriage is the civil status of one man and one woman united in law for life, for the discharge to each other and the community of the duties legally incumbent on those whose association is founded on the distinction of sex" (meaning male and female).

Prior to 2003, all dictionary definitions specified male and female. Some emphasized civil purposes, some religious purposes, or a combination of both. Some were written in a moralizing tone and included monogamy and propagation; others were more neutral and referenced civil commitment.

Dictionaries reflect the times in which they are written. The *Merriam-Webster's Collegiate Dictionary* (11th edition,

2003) was one of the first to add same-sex unions to its definition of marriage:

> (1) "the state of being united to a person of the opposite sex as husband or wife in a consensual and contractual relationship recognized by law; (2) the state of being united to a person of the same sex in a relationship like that of a traditional marriage."

In 2004, Massachusetts was the first state to legalize same-sex marriage. Connecticut would be the second state to do so in 2008. Iowa, Vermont, and New Hampshire followed in 2009.

The *Oxford English Dictionary* added same-sex to its definition of marriage in 2003, as well. It also included a definition of gay marriage, which traced the first use of the term back to 1971:

> "Gay Marriage n. relationship or bond between partners of the same sex which is likened to that between a married man and woman; a formal marriage bond contracted between two people of the same sex, often conferring legal rights; the action of entering into such a relationship; the condition of marriage between partners of the same sex."

Dictionaries have modified their definitions of marriage as social attitudes toward marriage have changed. As state Supreme Courts ruled that bans on same-sex marriage violated the constitutional rights of same-sex couples, dictionaries began adapting their definitions to reflect changing laws.

Purpose of Marriage

Determining the purpose of marriage is as individualized as it is institutionalized. Individuals may obviously subscribe to their own beliefs or reasons for marrying. Religious and civil institutions establish their purposes of marriage. If couples marry in a church, they agree to adhere to the purposes established by that religious institution. All marriages in the United States must be licensed and registered with the state in which the couples reside. They agree to abide by the criteria set forth by their state. Let's look at religious versus civil or secular purposes of marriage.

Religious

'To create a stable home in which children can grow and thrive. The best marriage is between two believers and one that can produce godly offspring."

Malachi 2:13–15 is often referenced.

Most Evangelical churches state that marriage is a union that covers every aspect of human existence: the physical, the sexual, the mental, the emotional, the moral, the spiritual, and the economic...summed up in the words of Genesis 2:24

(NKJV): "Therefore a man shall leave his father and mother and be joined to his wife, and they shall become one flesh."

According to the Roman Catholic Church: "God made marriage and laws concerning marriage when he created Adam and Eve[1]. For bringing children into the world and rearing them[2]. For mutual help of husband and wife (Genesis 2:18, 21–22)[3]. Valid marriage can only be broken by death—not civil government."

Genesis 1:28 (KJV) is often cited as a central purpose to marriage. "Be fruitful and multiply." Christian couples who are infertile or choose not to have offspring might take issue with propagation as a central purpose to marriage; likewise for gay and lesbian couples, who do not bring children into their marriage. Many Churches prefer their own doctrines and advocate that couples should be believers and hold membership in their respective institutions.

The debate over civil versus religious definitions and purposes of marriage often hinges on which should take precedent. "Does the state have the authority to change God's laws?" was asked on a religious Web site delineating the purpose of marriage. The answer was, "No, God's laws come before man's laws. The state can require licensure and registration, but the purpose of marriage is ultimately to glorify God since he made us for his glory" (Isaiah 43:7). The Web site went on to itemize that which does not glorify God. At the top of the list are homosexuality and same-sex couples.

The belief that God's law and the interpretation of that law supersedes state and federal laws is the basis for the conflict over the 2015 Supreme Court decision and subsequent legalization of same-sex marriage in all fifty states. Christians who believe that God's law—their personal and their Church's interpretation—overrides civil law have stood against gay marriage in their jobs as clerks of court, ministers, bakers, and florists.

The Nashville Statement, signed by an evangelical coalition of 150 ministers in August 2017, gives voice and mandate to parishioners who oppose homosexuality and gay marriage. The Statement was issued as a "Christian manifesto on human sexuality." Among the 14 Beliefs:

> "We deny that God has designed marriage to be a homosexual, polygamous or polyamorous relationship...[1] We also deny that marriage is a mere human contract rather than a covenant made before God...[2] The approval of 'homosexual immorality' is a sin."[3]

This manifesto takes the debate a step further by stating that not only is homosexuality a sin, but *approval* of homosexuality is also a sin. That puts Christians who may have accepted homosexual family members, friends, or congregants on notice if their acceptance or love is seen as *approval*. This conflict is playing out in Churches today.

I will address the polarization and confusion experienced in so many Churches regarding homosexuality in my final chapters.

Civil

The government assigns responsibilities and benefits to married couples. As a social and legal institution, civil marriage confers many rights, protections, and benefits—both legal and practical. Some of these vary from state to state, but the list typically includes tax, estate planning, housing, consumer, government, employment, death, medical, and family benefits. More detailed coverage of these benefits can be found further in this chapter, under Civil Rights.

The purposes of civil marriage also include children, family, love, companionship, commitment, continuity, permanence, economics, security, legal privileges, social status, and societal approval or validation. The list goes on and overlaps with religious purposes, as well. In regard to the commonality between opposite and same-sex marriages, religious or civil, Joe Biden said it well:

> "All marriages, at their root, are about the following question, 'Who do you love?'"[4]

Requirements and Restrictions

Most would agree that love should be the central reason for marrying, but it is obviously not a requirement. Under civil law, love, fidelity, religious affiliation, and morality are not used as criteria. Who would be called upon or have the right to develop such a checklist in a democracy?

Requirements designated by the government are: civil or religious officiant, signatures of the couple and witnesses on the license, and registration with the state, which signifies binding legal agreement. To obtain a marriage license, both parties must be of sound mind, unimpaired by alcohol or drugs, not coerced, not fraudulent, at the legal age of consent, and at least one party a U.S. citizen. A court of law would step in if any of these criteria are violated or challenged.

Historically, restrictions have been placed upon age, family relations, race, and sexual orientation. Age is still restricted across the U.S., at eighteen years old the minimum (sixteen or seventeen years old requires parental consent in some states). Consanguinity, marrying a blood relative, is illegal in most states. However, twenty states today allow marriage between first cousins, and all but five states allow marriage between second cousins. Race can no longer be used to restrict marriage. The 1967 *Loving v Virginia* Supreme Court decision ruled it unconstitutional to deny interracial couples the right to marry. Sexual orientation can no longer be used as a determinant for restriction. In 2015, the *Obergefell v Hodges* Supreme Court decision ruled it unconstitutional to deny same-sex couples the right to marry.

Right to Define

Not only is there disagreement over the definition of marriage but also over WHO has the right to define marriage. Whoever holds the right to define determines who is included in that definition, as well as who is excluded. The crux of the arguments for and against gay marriage rests on this aspect. The next section of this chapter will address the arguments against gay marriage. The concluding portion of the chapter will look at arguments that support gay marriage.

Should the federal government define marriage? Have they now or in the past? State governments? Churches? Tradition?

ARGUMENTS *AGAINST* GAY MARRIAGE

Tradition and the Church

"We're not antigay, we're pro-traditional marriage."

The United States has a tradition of defining marriage as between one man and one woman. Opponents of gay marriage argue that tradition should be honored and should set **legal precedent**. In June 2015, several Supreme Court justices wrote about this time-honored definition and questioned whether it should be changed or not. They pointed out that for over two hundred years in the U.S. and thousands of years throughout world history, marriage has been between one man and one woman.

An opposing question was asked during the *Obergefell v Hodges* proceedings. Was there a viable legal reason to uphold tradition that excluded gays and lesbians from marrying? The justices, in a five-to-four vote, determined that there was none.

The United States has a two-hundred-year history of slavery. The same argument was used by those who opposed the abolition of slavery—tradition. If it worked economically and socially for over 200 years, why change it? Of course, it did not *work* for the slaves, just as defining marriage as only between one man and one woman does not *work* for homosexuals.

Traditionally, marriage between a man and a woman has been considered **natural**, and marriage between same-sex couples, unnatural. Gay marriage opponents argue that nature favors heterosexual couples and, therefore, they should be the only couples allowed to marry. Texas congressmen Louie Gohmert said:

> "How about if we take four heterosexual couples and put them on an island where they have everything they need to live and exist, and we take four couples of just men and put them on an island where they have all they need to survive. Then let's take four couples of just women and let's come back in 100 years and see which one nature favors."[5]

Obviously, two men or two women cannot reproduce on their own, but reproduction has never been a requirement for marriage in the United States. Childless couples, regardless of their sexual orientation, cannot be denied the right to marry or to remain married.

"Traditionally, **Christianity has defined marriage** as the union of one man and one woman," said Marco Rubio during the 2016 presidential campaign. He explained that he supports the traditional definition of marriage "not because I seek to impose my view on others, and not because I seek to discriminate against anyone, but because I believe that the union of one man and one woman is a **special relationship** with an extraordinary record of success at raising children into strong and successful people. That special relationship deserves to be elevated and set apart in our laws."[6]

The relationship between one man and one woman *has* been elevated and set apart in our laws. Honor and respect for heterosexual couples are not diminished by including gays and lesbians in the definition of marriage. "Special" is subjective and should not be used to determine who qualifies to marry. Additionally, Mr. Rubio and many others claim that by supporting traditional marriage, they are not seeking to impose their views on others or to discriminate against anyone. They may not have that *intent*, but the result *is* an imposition of their view or definition, one that excludes homosexuals. That exclusion is discriminatory no matter the intent.

A final argument in favor of tradition and the Church is that the **government cannot redefine** what it did not create. Many Christians see marriage as a pre-political institution, one ordained and defined by God, and that the government does not have a right to define it or redefine it—unless it is legislated between one man and one woman, as in 1996's Defense of Marriage Act.

> "When a fellow like me looks at the landscape and sees the depravity, the perversion—redefining marriage and telling us that marriage is not between a man and a woman... It is nonsense."[7]
>
> —PHIL ROBERTSON

No one is saying that marriage is not between a man and a woman. But since 2015, it can also be between two men and two women. Marriage does not have to be redefined. The definition can be *expanded* to include gays and lesbians. In a vote to amend the definition of marriage in its *Book of Order*, the Presbyterian Church, in 2015, changed the language to read:

> "Marriage involves a unique commitment between two people, traditionally a man and a woman, to love and support each other for the rest of their lives."

The definition previously specified "between a man and a woman." By now stating marriage is between two people, and also acknowledging traditionally between a man and woman, both sides of the debate are honored.

Leave It to the States

"Marriage laws should be settled on the state level rather than federal level."[8]

—TED CRUZ

"I think it's a bad law for the following reason. If you want to change the definition of marriage then you need to go to state legislatures and get them to change it. Because states have always defined marriage."[9]

—MARCO RUBIO

"The United States Constitution says nothing about marriage. The issue of what relationships government recognizes as a marriage is a political question, not a constitutional one. States have always been able to determine who may legally marry in their states."[10]

—BRIAN BROWN

The states' rights versus federal rights, an age-old debate that can be traced to the founding of our nation. In 1860, the South declared states' rights over several issues, most predominantly the right of individual states to legally maintain slavery. A federal amendment to the Constitution overrode state constitutions by outlawing slavery near the end of the American Civil War in 1865. Southern states declared that the Thirteenth Amendment was unconstitutional for decades afterward. They claimed that the federal government did not have the right to outlaw slavery in their states.

But the federal government *does* have the right to over-rule state legislations and courts. A brief lesson in civics tells us that our three branches of government, the Executive, the Legislative, and the Judicial, were designed to hold checks and balances over each other at the federal and state levels. Fortunately, the Thirteenth Amendment to our Constitution ended slavery. Representatives and senators from the states narrowly passed the measure. Since the U.S. Constitution is the supreme law of the land, state rights are superseded by federal law.

The above Cruz, Rubio, and Brown quotes correctly reference the right of states to determine their own marriage laws. They maintain that right unless their state marriage laws, amendments, or Supreme Court decisions are ruled unconstitutional. In 1967, the U.S. Supreme Court ruled that states did not have the right to deny marriage or imprison interracial couples. In 2015, the Supreme Court determined that the constitutional rights of same-sex couples were violated by states with laws or amendments excluding them from marriage.

Five Robed Judges Shouldn't Decide for Millions

"If someone wants to change the marriage laws, I don't think it should be five unelected lawyers down in Washington."[11]

—Ted Cruz

"The Supreme Court's ruling in *Obergefell v Hodges* is a significant setback for all Americans who believe in the Constitution, the rule of law, democratic self-government, and marriage as the union of a man and a woman. The ruling is as clear an example of **judicial activism** as we've had in a generation. Nothing in the Constitution justified the redefinition of marriage by judges."[12]

—RYAN ANDERSON

The same accusations of judicial activism were made in 1954, after the Supreme Court overturned the 1896 *Plessy v Ferguson* decision, which greenlighted segregation. State laws legalizing segregation since 1896 were struck down by the Supreme Court in 1954 as unconstitutional. Southern states said the Supreme Court did not have the right to force them to change their state laws. Those same states cited judicial activism versus the will of the people of their states in the 1967 *Loving v Virginia* decision legalizing interracial marriage.

The nine justices of the United States Supreme Court are charged with *interpreting* the law. They do not *make* laws, as Ted Cruz implied in his quote. Any ruling of unconstitutionality requires states to change their laws. The Supreme Court did not directly redefine marriage. They ruled in a five-four decision that it is unconstitutional to deny same-sex couples the right to marry. Consequently, that ruling deemed unconstitutional any state laws and amendments designating marriage as only between a man and woman.

"We're not bound by what nine people say in perpetuity. The Court doesn't have the final word…the executive and legislative branches are obligated to challenge the judicial branch."[13]

—RICK SANTORUM

In a democracy, citizens have the right to petition their legislators to pass amendments or to take cases to court to appeal previous decisions. The FMA and MPA have been proposed. The Federal Marriage Amendment and the Marriage Protection Amendment would define marriage as a union of one man and one woman. These checks and balances will play out into the future.

It Is Unconstitutional

"It's unconscionable, unconstitutional and completely, absolutely un-American."[14]

—RYAN FISCHER

"My response to this decision was that it was illegitimate, it was lawless, it was utterly contrary to the Constitution and that we should fight to defend marriage on every front."[15]

—TED CRUZ

"It's a betrayal of our Constitution…I am utterly disgusted with the Republican governors who complied with the court's orders."[16]

—MIKE HUCKABEE

Huckabee addressed the Republican Party as a whole: "Grow a spine, show a modicum of knowledge about the way we govern ourselves, and lead, follow, or get the heck out of the way."[17]

In the wake of the 2015 *Obergefell v Hodges* decision, many Republicans declared that it was unconstitutional for the Supreme Court to overturn state amendments banning same-sex marriage. Nationwide, the average vote in favor of these bans was 67 to 33% over the previous decade. Of the ten states with the largest vote margin favoring a ban, Southern states made up nine, with Oklahoma being the tenth. The highest vote margin was in Mississippi, at 86 to 14% in favor of banning same-sex marriage.

I lived in the great State of Nevada from 2000–2017. I will use this state's history on marriage amendments and laws passed during this time. It mirrors much of what went on across the nation, in other states that banned same-sex marriage. The purpose of this section of my chapter is not to go in-depth into the legalities of the state arguments versus the Supreme Court decision, but to give clarification and a broad overview of key aspects of those arguments.

State Marriage Bans

"Only a marriage between a male and female person shall be recognized and given effect in this state."

The amendment to Nevada's constitution passed with 67% of the vote in 2002. A 2012 federal lawsuit filed on behalf of eight couples, *Sevcik v Sandoval*, argued that Nevada's law barring same-sex couples from marriage was harmful and unconstitutional. The claim was that the State of Nevada violated the Equal Protection Clause of the U.S. Constitution. The case also argued that registered domestic partnerships, which had been available in Nevada since 2009, were inadequate substitutes for marriage and constituted a second-class status. Plaintiffs stated:

> "This is the State of Las Vegas—the marriage capital of the world. It's high time that Nevada's lesbian and gay residents have the same right to marry as the quarter million visitors who wed in Las Vegas each year."
>
> "Nevada's antigay law is not supported by any rational basis, let alone a 'compelling government interest,' which is the legal test that we believe all antigay laws must survive in order to stay on the books."[18]

A Nevada judge ruled against the plaintiffs in favor of upholding the state's ban on same-sex marriage. He stated, "The maintenance of the traditional institution of civil marriage between one man and one woman is a legitimate state interest."

The decision was appealed to the United States Court of Appeals for the Ninth Circuit. In 2014, Republican governor Brian Sandoval removed Nevada's legal brief defending the ban, saying, "It has become clear that this case is no longer defensible in court."[19]

This scenario played out in several more states across

the country. It was only a matter of time before one of these lawsuits would be heard by the U.S. Supreme Court. As states adopted amendments banning gay marriage, lawsuits were filed on behalf of same-sex couples. State Supreme Courts heard the cases, sometimes ending it there, or appeals went to district courts. Governors often stepped in favoring the amendments, or some refusing to defend the bans. State by state, year by year, state Supreme Courts overturned their amendments. Thirty-six states legalized same-sex marriage by early 2015. Fourteen states still upheld their same-sex marriage bans when *Obergefell v Hodges* was decided by the U.S. Supreme Court in June 2015.

Supreme Court Ruling

In a five-to-four vote, the Supreme Court determined that the right to marry is guaranteed to same-sex couples by both the Due Process and Equal Protection Clauses of the Fourteenth Amendment. The Supreme Court listed four reasons why the fundamental right to marry applies to same-sex couples:

1. The right to personal choice regarding marriage is inherent in the concept of individual autonomy.
2. The right to marry is fundamental because it supports a two-person union unlike any other in its importance to the committed individuals, a principle applying equally to same-sex couples.

3. The fundamental right to marry safeguards children and families and thus draws meaning from related rights of childrearing, procreation, and education.

4. Marriage is a keystone of our social order, and there is no difference between same- and opposite-sex couples with respect to this principle; consequently, preventing same-sex couples from marrying puts them at odds with society, denies them countless benefits of marriage, and introduces instability into their relationships for no justifiable reason.[20]

It's Against My Religious Beliefs

Those who believe homosexuality is a sin oppose same-sex marriage. There are a host of sins mentioned in the Bible. Even if one religion, Christianity, were to be used as the basis for marriage rights, Christian denominations would not agree on that list of rights or restrictions. And which sins would prevent people from marrying? Only homosexuality? Alcoholism? Gluttony? Divorce? Drug addiction? Interracial marriage? Adultery? Premarital sex? Would non-Christians or those opposed to Christianity be allowed to marry?

I won't belabor my point. We all have the right to our own religious beliefs, to practice, to associate, to marry accordingly. But someone else's religious beliefs should not determine who any of us have the right to marry. Religion or being religious is not a legal prerequisite for marriage in the United States.

It Forces Christians to Accept, Serve, Officiate

During the *Obergefell v Hodges* hearings, Justice Antonia Scalia raised the concern that conservative ministers would be forced to marry same-sex couples. Justice Elena Kagan cited examples of Orthodox rabbis already allowed to refuse to marry non-Jews. Protestant couples cannot demand to be married by Catholic priests. Priests can require Catholic instruction and membership before they marry couples

The First Amendment has most often been interpreted as granting religious institutions the right to set their own requirements for marriage. Many Southern churches still refused to marry interracial couples after the 1967 *Loving v Virginia* Supreme Court decision. The dispute played out in the late 60s, with interracial couples being denied the right to marry by ministers and clerks of court. There were lawsuits, countersuits, appeals, and amendments proposed to stop interracial marriage—all based upon sincerely-held religious beliefs.

Similarly, religious beliefs about the sin of homosexuality and illegitimacy of same-sex marriage have been cited as reason to deny marrying and serving same-sex couples. There are court cases pending in California, Colorado, Kentucky, Minnesota, North Carolina, Oregon, South Carolina, Virginia, and Washington, to name a few. Ministers, clerks of court, judges, bakers, florists, and videographers have been sued or have filed lawsuits. State courts are grappling with these disputes across the nation.

Colorado bakery owner Jack Phillips's lawsuit reached the Supreme Court and was heard on December 5, 2017. Can individuals, churches, and businesses deny services based on their religious beliefs? Are the civil rights of homosexuals being violated by these entities when denied services? Where should the line be drawn in interpreting the First Amendment? Over the years, citizens have held religious beliefs that blacks were inferior to whites and should not be served. Or that mixed-race relationships were unnatural and sinful and should not be validated.

A conservative religious publication launched a movement in November 2014 to encourage pastors, as representatives of the state, to refuse to perform same-sex marriages. The "Marriage Pledge" was drafted by an ordained Anglican professor and an ordained Episcopal priest. "We the undersigned, commit ourselves to disengaging civil and Christian marriage."[21]

In December 2015, Mike Huckabee said he would "absolutely decline to enforce the marriage equality decision because it's a matter of saving our republic." He also ensured that, were he elected, his attorney general "would protect in every way the rights of those citizens who joined in disagreeing."[22]

This "I Stand with Phil Robertson" Facebook post characterizes the divide:

"We have a right to say what our beliefs are. Yes, I am a Christian. I believe the Bible. I do not support homosexuality or 'homosexual marriage.'"

"Yes, I still love you. Yes, we are still friends. No, I am not judging you. No, I am not condemning you to hell. No, I will not let anyone bully you."

"But realize that name-calling and stereotyping those of us who stand for what we believe is exactly what you don't want done to you. We have a right to speak what we believe, same as you have a right to speak what you believe."[23]

Yes, stereotyping and name-calling have no place in this debate. Yes, we all have the right to speak what we believe. The difference is that homosexuals' beliefs about marrying who they love does not directly impact conservative Christians. But Christians' beliefs against homosexuality and same-sex marriage can directly impinge on gays and lesbians—if it goes beyond stating belief to denial of services or membership in Churches.

We Must Stay Faithful to Christ's Teachings and the Sanctity of Marriage

"The nation must defend the sanctity of marriage."

—GEORGE W. BUSH, 2004 STATE OF
THE UNION ADDRESS

"Christ's teaching about these matters has become in our day a line in the sand – even among those who call themselves Christians. Already we have seen Christian leaders forsake Christ's teaching on marriage."[24]

—DENNY BURK

"RESOLVED, That Southern Baptists recognize no governing institution has the authority to negate or usurp God's definition of marriage."[25]

—RESOLUTION 5

It is natural that Christians advocate for Christ's teachings. As stated earlier, religions, specifically Christianity, do not determine who qualifies to marry in a democracy. They have the right to determine that within their own congregations, for those who adhere to their doctrines. And even among Christian denominations there is disagreement about Christ's teachings.

Jesus preached about marriage, divorce, and the role of males and females in Matthew 19:1–12. As was discussed in Chapter 4, marriage between men and women has been the *norm* throughout history. Jesus did not mention or condemn homosexual relations. There was no concept of sexual orientation and of loving and committed same-sex relationships during His day.

Reverend Mark Gallagher, a Unitarian minister, in 2004 asked what makes for sacredness in a marriage. He named four things:

1. Mutual love
2. Fidelity
3. Intimacy
4. Forgiveness

He further asked, "Why would we, as Americans, not want our government and its laws to recognize that same marriage sanctity for gay and lesbian individuals in their pursuit of liberty and happiness?"[26]

It Will Lead to Marrying Animals, Siblings, Laptops

"Watch what happens, love affairs between men and animals are going to be absolutely permitted. Polygamy, without question, is going to be permitted."[27]

—PAT ROBERTSON

"I'm opposed to the redefinition of a 5,000-year definition of marriage. I'm opposed to having a brother and sister being together and calling that marriage. I'm opposed to an older guy marrying a child and calling that marriage. I'm opposed to one guy having multiples wives and calling that marriage."[28]

—RICK WARREN

"Allowing same-sex couples to marry would lead to incestuous unions of couples such as mother and daughter, sister and sister, or brother and brother."[29]

—BISHOP ANTHONY TAYLOR

A Tennessee lawyer carried his challenge of same-sex marriage to courthouses across the nation. He filed a lawsuit in a Houston, Texas, federal court, saying "he and his 2011 MacBook were rejected for a marriage license in Harris

County."[30] He sued the district clerk, the Texas attorney general, and the governor, claiming his Fourteenth Amendment right to marry was denied. The cases in Tennessee, Utah, and Texas were eventually thrown out but drew much public attention in his campaign against gay marriage. The opposing Texas attorney asked for dismissal, arguing that the "U.S. Supreme Court's landmark Obergefell decision allowing same-sex marriage did not extend to man and machine."

It's a Slippery Slope to Debauchery and Moral Decay

"If the Supreme Court rules against marriage, all hell is going to break loose."[31]

—Tom DeLay

"I think there's an attempt to destroy the institution of marriage and I think it will cause, literally cause the destruction of our country."[32]

—Roy Moore

"The country can be no stronger than its families. I really believe if what the Supreme Court is about to do is carried through with, and it looks like it will be, then we're going to see a general collapse in the next decade or two."[33]

—James Dobson

"A new era of civil disobedience may be at hand."[34]

—Pat Buchanan

"If this court decides that they're going to change the definition of marriage, that then throws this country into an endless trauma."[35]

—Steve King

"This so-called lifestyle—I just can't believe it, they have tried to destroy marriage."[36]

—Pat Robertson

"The fact that we live in a society that can defend two men or two women entering a sexual relationship and, with wild inconceivability, call it marriage shows that the collapse of our culture into debauchery and anarchy is probably not far away."[37]

—John Piper

"Anybody who knows something about the history of the human race knows that there is no civilization which has condoned homosexual marriage widely and openly that has long survived."[38]

—Todd Akin

ARGUMENTS *FOR* GAY MARRIAGE

Who Does It Harm?

According to the above quotes, marriage as an institution will be destroyed. Our nation faces anarchy, debauchery, trauma, and inevitable collapse. All pretty serious claims at the hands of the Supreme Court and same-sex marriage. Time will tell, but let's look at who is directly harmed by homosexuals marrying. The government? The Churches? Heterosexual couples? Marriage itself? I have searched high and low, read, researched, talked with those who are antigay marriage and pro-gay marriage. I am still not able to verify any direct damage. Theoretically, philosophically, theologically perhaps—but all based from opinion and inter-pretation, with no substantial examples.

How would my marriage to another woman directly impact anyone else's marriage? How does who I love or who I marry affect heterosexual couples or the institution of mar-riage as a whole? The above claims serve to sensationalize, polarize, and stir fear. There is no proof in the three years since *Obergefell v Hodges* that gay marriage harms Christians or their marriages, or that it causes fewer heterosexual mar-riages, or directly damages anyone. Homosexuals' belief in the right to marry does not take away heterosexuals' right to marry. Conservative Christians' belief that it is sinful and wrong for gays to marry *does* take away the right for homo-sexuals to marry. Banning same-sex marriage prior to 2015 harmed gays and lesbians.

There are those who feel their religious beliefs are vio-lated if forced to officiate, bake a cake, or provide flowers for a same-sex ceremony. This chapter opened with the debate over religious belief and the right to marry. Chapter 9 will explore more in-depth that debate and pending court cases across the nation.

It Is a Civil Right

"RESOLVED, That the messengers to the Southern Baptist Convention meeting in New Orleans, Louisiana, June 19–20, 2012, oppose any attempt to frame 'same-sex marriage' as a civil rights issue."

"RESOLVED, That we deny that the effort to legalize 'same-sex marriage' qualifies as a civil rights issue since homosexuality does not qualify as a class meriting special protections, like race and gender."

"RESOLVED, That we encourage Southern Baptists everywhere to fight for the civil rights of all people where such rights are consistent with the righteousness of God."

The caveat, homosexuals are not consistent with the righteousness of God, according to Southern Baptists. Therefore, their right to marry should not be granted and should not be considered a civil right.

The U.S. Supreme Court ruled otherwise. The issue was not about placing homosexuality into a "class meriting special protections." The Court's decision centered around marriage as a civil right.

"The right to personal choice regarding marriage is inherent in the concept of individual autonomy... Marriage is a keystone of our social order... Preventing same-sex couples from marrying puts them at odds with society, denies them countless benefits of marriage."[39]

There are hundreds of rights or benefits to marriage that heterosexual couples have always received. These rights now extend to same-sex couples. A few examples: filing joint income tax returns; inheriting a share of a spouse's estate; obtaining priority if a spouse needs a conservator; receiving Social Security, Medicare, and disability benefits for a spouse; receiving veterans' and military benefits for spouses; obtaining insurance benefits through a spouse's employer; family leave to care for a spouse in illness; visiting a spouse in a hospital intensive care unit; making medical decisions if a spouse is incapacitated; making burial arrangements; adopting children; receiving family rates for insurances. Gay and lesbian couples lived without these rights prior to the legalization of same-sex marriage.

Why Do We Need to Approve of Someone Else's Marriage?

I understand the deeply-held beliefs that many Christians have about homosexuality and gay marriage. My question, however, is: Why do we need to get into the business of approving or disapproving anyone else's marriage? As a Christian, I have certain beliefs on what constitutes a healthy and committed marriage. I believe in fidelity, responsibility, accountability, and shared beliefs and values. I would not think of imposing my beliefs onto someone else's marriage or begin to think that I should determine who is allowed to marry.

Why Should the Government End Gay Marriage?

The right to marry has been granted to gays and lesbians nationwide. In order for Congress to put forward an amendment to the Constitution to take that right away, they must prove it is in the government's best interest to do so. Or they must prove the harm of gay marriage to individuals and society. The Supreme Court determined that it was harmful and unconstitutional to *deny* homosexuals the right to marry.

Why Should I Not Have the Right to Marry?

Again, I understand the interpretation of the Bible that says that I am in sin, that I am condemned to Hell, and that I cannot marry a woman. If you hold that belief based on your Christian faith, I still ask, "Can you honestly tell me I should not have the right to choose who to marry, and that YOU do have that right? In a democracy? Where I am an educated, responsible, law-abiding, tax-paying citizen? You should have that right based on your religious beliefs, but I should not?" Imagine if the tables were turned, that you could not marry the man or woman you love because of someone else's religious beliefs.

"How can the law grant the right of marriage to prison inmates but not to two responsible women?"[40]

—Fenton Johnson

Regardless which side of the marriage debate someone is on, emotions run high. Gays and lesbians feel strongly about having the right to marry stripped from them, having their current marriages invalidated, or being denied services as couples. Conservative Christians feel as strongly about their biblical beliefs, defining marriage as only between a man and a woman, and overturning gay marriage.

Two colliding beliefs and outcomes. Gays and lesbians, their families, Churches, the political arena are all adversely impacted when there is no resolution. An *us vs them* mentality has permeated and divided our society.

The next chapter will explore religious freedom advocacy since the 2015 *Obergefell v Hodges* Supreme Court decision. Variations of Religious Freedom Restoration Acts have been passed in 21 states. Numerous lawsuits at the local and state levels have been filed across the country. Most of these court cases are centered around the right of religious organizations and public businesses to act in accordance with their "sincerely-held" religious beliefs regarding homosexuality and same-sex marriage. Gays and lesbians have countered with lawsuits claiming discrimination based on their sexual orientation. A Colorado bakers' lawsuit culminated in a Supreme Court hearing and decision. Masterpiece Cakeshop v Colorado Civil Rights Commission exemplifies arguments on all sides of the religious freedom debate. This case will be covered in-depth in Chapter 9.

CHAPTER 9

Religious Freedom

There is currently much debate over religious freedom and the right to refuse service to gays and lesbians when it runs contrary to beliefs about homosexuality and same-sex marriage. Let's take a look at the core beliefs and values of those advocating for religious freedom—a principle central to our Constitution and democracy.

United States Constitution

Amendment 1

Congress shall make no law respecting an establishment of religion, or prohibiting the free exercise thereof; or abridging the freedom of speech, or of the press; or the right of the people peaceably to

assemble, and to petition the Government for a redress of grievances.

The Bill of Rights, the first ten amendments to our Constitution, was ratified in 1791. Individual rights were delineated and guaranteed, but not universally agreed upon over the next two centuries.

That is the beauty of our democracy. In a sense, the three branches "duke it out" when laws or amendments are passed, rights are denied or granted, and individuals or groups disagree with the results. Some say justice can be swayed by the prevailing winds of liberalism or conservatism, depending on which political party is in office, who controls Congress, and in which direction the Supreme Court is *stacked*. Very rarely are both parties happy or in agreement. The commonality is that the electorate speaks in any given year, decade, or century. Majority rules—and those who vote elect presidents, senators, and representatives. Although Supreme Court justices are not directly elected, presidents who nominate them are, and legislators who confirm them.

The First Amendment, oft cited in lawsuits, has withstood the test of time. It is beautifully worded, hotly debated, and central to disagreements and tensions around religious freedom today. "Congress shall make no law respecting an establishment of religion, or prohibiting the free exercise thereof."

No surprise that both sides of the debate refer to the First Amendment. Those who advocate for gay marriage, and the right to be served by businesses regardless of their sexual orientation, argue that there should be *no establishment of religion* by the government. In other words, Christianity and its anti-homosexual stance should not be foundational to determining the definition of marriage and who is allowed to marry.

Christians who believe homosexuality is an abomination, and that same-sex marriage is sinful and invalid, argue that their rights are violated when forced to bake or design a cake, to provide flowers, to cater, or to hire out as photographers for gay weddings. If not allowed to conscientiously deny services for same-sex marriages, these businesses feel that their *free exercise of religion is being prohibited.*

MASTERPIECE CAKESHOP v COLORADO CIVIL RIGHTS COMMISSION

The free exercise of religion was fundamental to the lawsuit filed on behalf of bakery owner Jack Phillips. It was heard by the Supreme Court on December 5, 2017 with a decision handed down on June 4, 2018. Both sides were convinced of their legal rightness and the violation of their individual rights.

This was a tough one for me personally. As a Christian, I hold dearly the right to freely practice and express my religious beliefs. As a lesbian, I hold dearly the right to marry and to be served in any establishment, regardless of my sexual orientation. Having said that, I have perused countless articles and read up on every detail about this case. In fact,

I just purchased cookies from Jack Phillips at his cake shop in Lakewood, Colorado near my home. A kind man, great little bakery, two containers at the counter were designated for donations. One marked for individual expenses for Mr. Phillips and the other for the organization representing his case—Alliance Defending Freedom. Much time, money, and energy has been put into this lawsuit since two gay men requested a custom-designed cake in April 2012.

Background

Charlie Craig and David Mullins came into Masterpiece Cakeshop to purchase a custom-designed wedding cake for their upcoming ceremony. Jack Phillips offered to sell them any pre-baked cake in the store, but said he could not custom-design a cake for a same-sex ceremony. Reportedly, the two men left in a huff and proceeded to file a complaint with the Colorado Civil Rights Commission.

Mr. Phillips received a notice from the commission, stating that he was in violation of state civil rights laws, had discriminated against the gay couple, and would be required to bake and design cakes for homosexual weddings in the future. He would also be under a two-year inspection, which would assure the state of his compliance.

The American Civil Liberties Union (ACLU) stepped in to represent the gay couple. The Alliance Defending Freedom (ADF) took the owner's case. Both sides claimed that the other was deliberately exaggerating the situation and looking for a fight; that Craig and Mullins sought out a bakery that would not take their order to prove a point about discrimination; that Phillips singled out the gay couple in his opposition to same-sex marriage to prove a point about religious freedom. Regardless, both sides felt strongly about their case, found representation, sued, countersued, and appealed all the way to the Supreme Court.

Arguments

Hostility Toward Religion

During the December 5th Supreme Court hearing, Justice Anthony Kennedy questioned whether the Colorado Civil Rights Commission was tolerant or respectful of Mr. Phillips's religious beliefs or not. The ADF, on behalf of Phillips, had appealed their case in 2015 to the CCRC but were refused a hearing. A statement issued by the commission said, "Using religion to justify discrimination is a despicable piece of rhetoric."[1] The ADF asserted that the commission exhibited an anti-religious bias in its refusal to hear their appeal.

Artistic Exception for Bakers

"The government should not force anyone to create art that conflicts with their conscience."[2] Jack Philips said that he did not want his creative talents channeled toward an activity (same-sex marriage) that was against his conscience. His legal team claimed that a baker who custom-designs cakes is an artist and artists have the right to free expression. During the Supreme Court hearing, it was asked whether or not restaurant owners and cooks are also artists, and should be able to deny services based on their religious beliefs. Hairstylists, photographers, florists? Where should the line be drawn?

Restaurant owners in the South denied services to blacks due to their conscience and a belief that blacks were inferior. The 1964 Civil Rights Act ruled that denial of service was illegal.

Phillips Did Not Refuse Service to Gays, He Refused to Celebrate Same-Sex Marriage

Phillips offered other cakes in his shop to Craig and Mullins. He had served gays in the past. It was the request for a custom-designed cake that, as an artist, ran contrary to his Christian convictions. He did not want to be party to celebrating same-sex marriage, which he believed was unholy and sinful. "It was the message, not the people." He said he did not discriminate against two gay men; he stood by his religious belief that same-sex marriage is wrong.[3]

Under public accommodation laws, all customers should have the same access to products or services sold in businesses. At Masterpiece Cakeshop, only pre-baked wedding cakes were offered to the gay couple. Pre-baked AND custom-designed cakes were regularly offered to heterosexuals.

The Right to Refuse Service

"No Shirt, No Shoes, No Service"
"We Reserve the Right to Refuse Service to Anyone"
Are these signs legal?

If a business owner determines that lack of shoes or shirt poses a danger to the patrons, or if it's merely enough to make others uncomfortable, these signs are both legal and completely justified. If clothing requirements are geared toward a specific group, it can become a problem.

Under federal anti-discrimination laws, businesses can refuse service to any person for any reason, unless the business is discriminating against a protected class. At the *national* level, *protected class* includes: race or color, national origin or citizenship status, religion or creed, gender, disability, pregnancy, veteran status.

Some *states*, like California and Colorado, go beyond the federal list to include: marital status, sexual orientation or gender identity, medical condition, political affiliation.

Businesses can post signs that they reserve the right to refuse service to customers. They can legally deny service if someone is nude, barefoot, using inflammatory speech, threatening, or violent. Of course, the legality of that refusal is often challenged and determined in local courts.

Jewish restaurant owners or butchers do not serve pork because it is not kosher and runs contrary to their religious beliefs. But they do not offer pork *equally* to all customers.

They do not advertise pork products, but a baker does advertise wedding cakes.

Bakers, printers, and engravers have refused to put hate speech on their products. A Denver bakery in 2014 refused to make a cake with an antigay message. The Colorado Civil Rights Commission ruled that the bakery did not discriminate. The customer requested a cake in the shape of a Bible with "Homosexuality is a detestable sin, Leviticus 18:22" written on it. He may appeal the CCRC's decision.

Walmart refused to bake a cake with a confederate flag. The case was upheld in a local court. Should a black carpenter be forced to make a cross for the Ku Klux Klan? Should a Jewish caterer be required to serve at a Moslem event? It's highly unlikely that these two requests would be made in the first place. Should a Christian have the right to refuse service to an atheist or an atheist refuse a Christian? This line of questioning is endless.

The KKK is not a protected class. Race and religion are protected. Sexual orientation is a protected class in the State of Colorado. The CCRC cited this in their initial ruling against the Masterpiece Cakeshop. Only twenty-one other states include sexual orientation as protected.

In the Masterpiece Cakeshop case, the ADF made a distinction that Phillips was not "discriminating against an entire class of people but was conscientiously objecting to a particular kind of ceremony."[4]

There Is No Evidence that the Gay Couple Could Not Find Another Wedding Cake Vendor

It is true that in most cities, any gay couple would have the option of finding another bakery that might custom-design their cake. But should they have to? Rural areas would be limited in bakery selections. It is one thing if a business does not have the ingredients or the artistic design that a couple is looking for and they choose to go elsewhere. It is another if a bakery advertises wedding cakes and will custom-design for some customers but not others.

Public Accommodation Laws

"All persons shall be entitled to the full and equal enjoyment of the goods, services, facilities, and privileges, advantages, and accommodations of any place of public accommodation, as defined in this section, without discrimination or segregation on the ground of race, color, religion, or national origin."

—CIVIL RIGHTS ACT OF 1964 (TITLE II)

A place of public accommodation would include "operations that affect commerce"—lodgings, restaurants, medical, retail establishments, gas stations, theaters. The list goes on.

Hearing Summary

Religious freedom should be upheld. Jack Phillips and the ADF argued that it was within his rights as a Christian, a business owner, and an artist to refuse to design a cake for Charlie Craig and David Mullins. His refusal was not in opposition to their sexual orientation but to same-sex marriage. He was willing to sell them a pre-baked cake. The couple also had the option to purchase a custom cake at a number of bakeries nearby. Phillips experienced hardship and discrimination when the CCRC ruled that he was in violation and mandated that he design cakes for same-sex weddings in the future or face debilitating fines. He was also forced to provide comprehensive staff training and file quarterly compliance reports to the CCRC. Phillips's right to respectfully express his religious convictions in his own business was denied.

Anti-discrimination laws should be upheld. A bakery must abide by public accommodation laws and provide services equally to all of its customers. Craig and Mullins were denied a custom-designed cake that was regularly offered to heterosexuals. They were discriminated against because of their sexual orientation. Opposing same-sex marriage is equivalent to opposing homosexuals. Sexual orientation is a protected class in the State of Colorado. Homosexuals should have the same access to goods and services as heterosexuals and should not be denied due to someone else's religious convictions.

Supreme Court Decision

In a 7-2 vote, the nation's highest court ruled that the State of Colorado violated the Free Exercise Clause of the First Amendment. The Commission's treatment of Phillips' case violated the State's duty under the First Amendment not to base laws or regulations on hostility to a religion or religious viewpoint. The Court overturned the Colorado Civil Rights Commission's ruling against Masterpiece Cakeshop owner, Jack Phillips.

The Supreme Court determined:

1. Phillips received "different treatment" than three other Colorado bakers who the Commission allowed to decline creating cakes they deemed offensive.
2. There was evidence of "hostility" and "clear bias" against Phillips' Christian beliefs.
3. Phillips' decisions were understandable in 2012 when same-sex marriage was not yet legal in Colorado.

The majority opinion written by Justice Anthony Kennedy stated:[5]

1. "The State Civil Rights Division concluded in at least three cases that a baker acted lawfully in declining to create cakes with decorations that demeaned gay persons or gay marriages. Phillips too was entitled to

a neutral and respectful consideration of his claims in all the circumstances of the case."

2. "One commissioner suggested that Phillips can believe 'what he wants to believe,' but cannot act on his religious beliefs 'if he decides to do business in the state.' The commissioner even went so far as to compare Phillips' invocation of his sincerely held religious beliefs to defenses of slavery and the Holocaust. This sentiment is inappropriate for a Commission charged with the solemn responsibility of fair and neutral enforcement of Colorado's antidiscrimination law – a law that protects discrimination on the basis of religion as well as sexual orientation... The commission showed a clear and impermissible hostility toward the sincere religious beliefs motivating his objection."

3. "His (Jack Phillips) dilemma was understandable in 2012, which was before Colorado recognized the validity of gay marriages performed in the State and before this Court issued United States v. Windsor. Given the State's position at the time, there is some force to Phillips' argument that he was not unreasonable in deeming his decision lawful."

Justice Kennedy also stated that "the outcome of cases like this in other circumstances must await further elaboration in the courts, all in the context of recognizing that these disputes must be resolved with tolerance, without undue disrespect to sincere religious beliefs, and without subjecting gay persons to indignities when they seek goods and services in an open market."[6]

RELIGIOUS FREEDOM vs ANTI-DISCRIMINATION LAWS

Courts across the country are attempting to strike that balance between "respecting sincere religious beliefs and not subjecting gays and lesbians to indignities when they seek goods and services." Similar scenarios to Colorado have played out in other states and their court systems.

Most notable was in <u>Kentucky</u>, when court clerk Kim Davis refused to issue a marriage license to two men in July 2015. Just days after the *Obergefell v Hodges* Supreme Court ruling, the incident was widely covered in the news. Former Arkansas governor Mike Huckabee stood with Kim Davis at the courthouse after she spent several days in jail. Huckabee represented the voice of religious freedom and advocated for the right of Christians to stand against same-sex marriage based on religious convictions. Davis's lawyers claimed that her rights and First Amendment freedom were "substantially burdened."

The governor of <u>Mississippi</u> signed the "Protecting Freedom of Conscience from Government Discrimination Act" in April 2016. The bill protects by law the belief that marriage is the union of one man and one woman. It prevents government intervention when Churches or businesses act "based upon or in a manner consistent with a sincerely held religious belief or moral conviction."[7] Opponents of the bill said that the law amounted to state sanction for open discrimination. Lawsuits and appeals have been filed with state and district courts. The controversial House Bill 1523 remains a law in Mississippi.

Indiana conservative advocacy groups filed a lawsuit against several city anti-discrimination ordinances in August 2016. In response, the Indiana legislators passed Bill 101, titled the Religious Freedom Restoration Act (RFRA), which allows individuals and companies to "assert that their exercise of religion has been substantially burdened"[8] as a defense in legal proceedings.

Twenty-one states have some version of the Religious Freedom Restoration Act in place:

AL, AZ, AR, CT, FL, ID, IL, IN, KS, KY, LA, MS, MO, NM, OK, PA, RI, SC, TN, TX and VA.

Twenty-two states, the District of Columbia, Guam, and Puerto Rico have passed anti-discrimination statutes that protect against sexual orientation discrimination:

CA, CO, CT, DE, HA, IL, IA, ME, MD, MA, MN, NH, NV, NJ, NM, NY, OR, RI, UT, VT, WA, WI

The Religious Freedom Restoration Act was originally passed at the federal level by Congress in 1993. Congressman Chuck Schumer (D-NY) and Senator Ted Kennedy (D-MA) introduced the bill in opposition to a Supreme Court decision upholding the firing of two Native-American drug rehabilitation counselors who had ingested peyote during religious ceremonies. With strong bi-partisan support it cleared the Senate 97-3 and passed unopposed in the House. The purpose of the Act was to "protect religious individuals and organizations against government interference with the practice of their faith."

There are Religious freedom laws in twenty-one states. Anti-discrimination laws protecting sexual orientation in twenty-two states. Some believe these respective laws are on a collision course. **Can states protect against sexual-orientation discrimination without compromising religious freedom?** Many had hoped the Supreme Court would definitively answer that in *Masterpiece Cakeshop v Colorado Civil Rights Commission.* State supreme courts across the country are dealing with similar lawsuits. It may be only a matter of time before another case reaches the Supreme Court.

OPPOSITION TO SAME-SEX MARRIAGE

Businesses

A majority of the recent religious freedom court cases have centered around the right to oppose gay marriage. Most lawsuits have been filed on behalf of businesses that provide services for wedding ceremonies—bakeries, florists, caterers, and photographers. Of particular note are three recent cases on the West Coast:

A judge in Bakersfield, <u>California</u>, ruled in February 2018 that Tastries Bakery owner could continue to refuse to make wedding cakes for same-sex couples, and that artistic expression and sincerely-held religious beliefs were protected by the First Amendment. The judge said the difference in this case was that the cake in question had not yet been baked and the owner "should not be compelled to use her talents to design and create a cake in celebration of a marital union her religion forbids."[9] Another bakery had been recommended to the lesbian couple. The ruling is being appealed.

An Oregon appeals court upheld a $135,000 judgment against the Christian owners of Sweetcakes by Melissa in December 2017. Arguments made by both sides were similar to the Masterpiece Cakeshop case. Additionally, the lesbian couple sued for emotional damages, claiming that the owners had exposed their names and address on Facebook postings of court documents. Both sides experienced harassment and death threats. Because of the $135,000 judgment, the owners were financially forced to close their shop. They may appeal to the Oregon Supreme Court or await the anticipated June 2018 U.S. Supreme Court decision.

The ADF filed *Arlene's Flowers v State of Washington* with the Supreme Court in July 2017. The owner had served and employed gays and lesbians previously, but said she could not use her creative skills to beautify the same-sex ceremony of a long-time customer. Gay couples most often cite public accommodation laws in their request to be served by businesses. However, religious organizations and private clubs are generally exempt from public accommodation requirements.

Churches

Can Ministers Be Forced to Marry Same-Sex Couples?

Ministers opposed to same-sex marriage **cannot** be forced to marry same-sex couples. Worries and fears that ministers could be forced fueled even more antigay marriage sentiment following the *Obergefell v Hodges* ruling in 2015. After much research, I have come across only one case where it was *reported* that two ministers would be forced to marry homosexuals under threat of shutting down their chapel. Rumors spread in the midst of national news coverage in October 2014—six months before the *Obergefell v Hodges* ruling.

Idaho's state ban on same-sex marriage had just been struck down by a federal court. A gay couple inquired about a ceremony at the Hitching Post Wedding Chapel in Coeur d'Alene. Worried they would be forced to marry the couple, the owners closed down the chapel for several days. The story quickly drew national attention, but there was no basis for the owners' fears. Both were ordained ministers and the chapel was registered as a religious organization. They were never threatened, fined, or forced to marry anyone. The Alliance Defending Freedom (ADF) filed a suit on behalf of the owners, alleging the city's nondiscrimination laws violated their religious freedom and that they had lost money after closing their chapel. A judge dismissed most of the suit except for a portion seeking $1,000 in damages for the time the chapel was closed.

Notable among state Supreme Court cases, a 1985 *State v Barclay* ruling in Kansas determined that the state could not tell a minister how to conduct religious worship or ceremonies.

Leaders of the Southern Baptist Convention, after the *Obergefell v Hodges* decision, said that they did not see the ruling as posing a direct threat to pastors. "I am not aware of any problem of a pastor being coerced to conduct a same-sex marriage," said Roger Oldham, spokesman for the SBC.[10]

"The Constitution makes clear that churches don't have to marry anyone. And the American Civil Liberties Union (ACLU) would defend any cleric who faces such a threat from the government."[11]

—JAMES ESSEKS

Marriage Amendment Proposals

Many of the states with religious freedom laws have also proposed state marriage amendments to nullify same-sex marriage. There are currently no states with enough political traction to pass an amendment. At the national level, the last congressional vote for the Federal Marriage Amendment took place in 2006. It defined marriage as a union between one man and one woman, but lost in the House of Representatives 236 to 187. The FMA was last proposed in 2015. It did not garner enough support to make it out of committee.

Businesses, Churches, court cases, state same-sex marriage bans, Religious Freedom Restoration Acts, federal marriage amendment proposals—all seeking to nullify, invalidate, refuse to participate in, or recognize same-sex marriage.

My Question

Why such strong opposition to same-sex marriage? I ask that sincerely *and* rhetorically. Why such vehemence and resolve to end gay marriage? Yes, based upon conviction and religious belief. But why does that conviction or disqualification not extend to other sins or aspects of marriage? Jack Phillips deems homosexuality and same-sex marriage to be sinful and unholy. Does he also not design cakes for those couples who are guilty of the sin of infidelity, addiction, abuse, lack of commitment to each other, divorce, or lack of respect for Christianity or any religion? There are so many "unholy" relationship possibilities that couples may bring to a business transaction. Where do owners with religious convictions draw the line? How far do they extend their discomfort or judgment?

As the debate continues, the divide between Christians and homosexuals deepens. The following chapter examines the impact of anti-homosexuality and same-sex marriage religious beliefs on gays and lesbians.

CHAPTER 10

WHY IT MATTERS

When individuals believe, and Churches preach, that homosexuality is an abomination, it matters. When an entire demographic is targeted as going to Hell, in need of redemption, and are required to "change" their sexual orientation in order to be accepted or remain in good standing, it matters. It matters to those who have lost their families, communities, and Churches—to those who have been subjected to conversion therapy, required to remain celibate, or to deny their sexual orientation. It also matters to the friends, family, and church members of gays and lesbians who have been condemned and rejected, most often in the name of God and love.

Little wonder there is such a divide in our society and in our churches. **How do God-fearing, sincere, Bible-believing Christians shore up their interpretation of Scriptures with everyday encounters with gays and**

lesbians? So many are torn between their love for someone who is gay and accepting or welcoming them in the face of strongly-held beliefs against homosexuality. These inner and outer conflicts play out in families, congregations, in the workplace, and in businesses.

I have offered my answers throughout this book—and I will conclude in the final chapter with visions of hope, steps to take, and strategies to address this divide.

A sampling of <u>my answers</u> as I begin this chapter:

1. Read this book. Argue with it, disagree, or change your mind.
2. Read up on sexual orientation in Chapter 5. Understand what it is and what it is not.
3. Examine the Scriptures that have been used to condemn homosexuals in Chapter 4. Pray about it. Confirm your interpretation that it is sinful, admit you're not sure, or change your mind.
4. Challenge your assumptions about gays and lesbians by reading Chapter 6, on stereotyping.
5. Look at the arguments for and against gay marriage in Chapter 8. Ask yourself why you believe what you believe and how that should impact homosexuals in your life.
6. No matter your stance or biblical interpretation, be on the side of empathy, compassion, and kindness.

How do we get beyond the disagreements, divisiveness, posturing, entrenchment, and polarization we see playing out in our society today? **I suggest that no matter which side you are on, there is benefit to educating yourself on the beliefs and experiences of those with whom you disagree.**

When Christians believe that the Bible condemns homosexuality, they must decide how to treat homosexuals in their Churches, families, workplaces, and businesses. Some choose to reject, condemn, excommunicate, or enforce celibacy or reparative therapy. This chapter will look at the impact of these harmful responses on gays and lesbians. Others voice their beliefs, may show love and acceptance, but insist that their own rights are violated when they are forced by state anti-discrimination laws to serve homosexuals or participate in same-sex weddings.

HOW OPPOSITION TO SAME-SEX MARRIAGE IMPACTS LESBIANS AND GAYS

The concerted effort through courts, legislation, businesses, and Churches to end gay marriage, to condemn it, to refuse to recognize it or to participate in it directly affects gays and lesbians. Weddings signify joy, celebration, family, community, and commitment. All are positive attributes ignored or still considered sinful or unholy because of the biblical interpretation of conservative Christians.

Objecting to who a family member or friend marries is nothing new. The objection may be based on religion, race, age, income, education, past, or personality. Those who love the couple have to decide whether or not to be welcoming despite their disapproval. Opposition to homosexuality and same-sex marriage carries with it a judgment beyond these other objections. Accusations of sin, unholiness, and hell carry much deeper criticism and condemnation.

Many concerned Christians are determined to end gay marriage. They attend Churches that preach its illegitimacy, donate to organizations that are fighting it at the state and federal levels, and they support politicians who are determined to overturn *Obergefell v Hodges*.

How would that not adversely affect gays and lesbians? What would the outcome be for homosexuals if Christians were successful in making same-sex marriage illegal? Gay couples and their children would be devastated to be stripped of legal recognition and rights. To be honest, I find it perplexing that loving and sincere Christians want to revoke a right they themselves enjoy. Overturning *Obergefell v Hodges* would be the first time in our nation's history that a Supreme Court decision would revoke rights that it previously granted and had determined were constitutional.

The Constitution ensures the right to religious freedom and expression. The First Amendment invokes the right to believe, express, and practice one's religion. The Fourteenth Amendment ensures "equal protection of the laws." Local, state, and federal courts interpret and determine when rights should be upheld or if discrimination occurs. *Masterpiece Cakeshop v Colorado Civil Rights Commission* showcases the complexities of this debate.

HOW <u>OPPOSITION TO HOMOSEXUALITY</u> IMPACTS LESBIANS AND GAYS

Most would agree that discriminating against people because of their religious beliefs *or* sexual orientation is wrong. Religious freedom advocates would argue that if a florist or cake designer is required by law to service a same-sex wedding, they experience discrimination because of their religious beliefs. I understand that it is a matter of principle, but what is the worst thing that could happen? Discomfort, prayer for forgiveness if being forced by law, or compassion in the midst of disagreement?

Those who were first forced by law to provide services to interracial couples felt that their religious conviction over the sin of mixed-race marriage was violated. Not to minimize any discomfort, but their lives went on. Providing services in those cases was a brief moment in their lifetime. Again, I realize that many feel strongly about not compromising their religious convictions. That is part of the reason why I am writing this book: to provide new information, to advocate for compassion, and to ask, WWJD (What would Jesus do?).

The First Amendment guarantees the right to religious belief, expression, and practice. What happens when religious practice or action negatively affects or discriminates against someone else? Gays or lesbians who marry or believe that homosexuality is not a sin do not negatively impact Christians who believes it *is* a sin. But Christians who believe that homosexuality is an abomination *have* adversely impacted homosexuals—in the workplace and housing, within Churches and families.

Jobs and Housing

States that protect homosexual employees from discrimination are in the minority. Gays and lesbians can still be fired or denied housing in twenty-eight states. Research conducted by the Center for American Progress showed that "LGBT people across the country continue to experience pervasive discrimination that negatively impacts all aspects of their lives."[1] While much progress has been made over the last decade, one in four reported experiencing discrimination in hiring, termination, promotion, and workplace harassment. A 2017 national survey and interviews revealed that LGBT people hide relationships, delay health care, change the way they dress, and take other steps to alter their lives to avoid discrimination.

Many businesses are adopting their own protective policies. Out & Equal recently reported: "In 1996, only 4% of Fortune 500 companies welcomed LGBT people with inclusive policies and protections. Today 92% of those companies do."[2] That clearly is progress on the business front. Advocates are working at the state levels to bring about increased fairness and parity.

Churches and Families

<u>Demands</u>

To remain in good standing within Churches and families that believe homosexuality is an abomination, gays and lesbians are expected to:

1. deny their homosexuality,
2. end their love relationship,
3. change their sexual orientation, and
4. become celibate.

Acceptance and inclusion in these families and Churches carry a heavy price. Those who interpret Scriptures as condemning of homosexuals may be compassionate and understanding in their requests or demands. They hold a sincere belief that their loved one or church member's salvation is at stake.

Chapter 5 looked at sexual orientation and the preponderance of evidence that it cannot be changed. Conversion therapy has not been proven to be effective. Ex-gay ministries have closed and apologized for promoting and enforcing it. Yet there are those who still believe in its effectiveness.

It is not my place to deny anyone else's experience. If people believe that their sexual orientation did change, no one should judge. Emily Thomes posted a video on Facebook in December 2017, telling her story of conversion and leaving homosexuality. She has been interviewed by several Christian organizations.

> "(The second) concern I see is when Christians cast aside what His word says on homosexuality in attempts to 'love' those who are lost. God's word stands forever; what He deems as sin will always be sin. To ignore that truth is incredibly unloving. Those who do not repent will not inherit the kingdom of God. Pretending that one can remain in sin and belong to Him is deceptive and cruel."[3]

Emily is decisive in her statements about homosexuality and sin. She has every right to ask that her own testimony and experience be heard, but she invalidates the testimony of Christian gays and lesbians by asserting that they cannot "remain in sin" and belong to Him. Her beliefs are based on *her* interpretation of the Bible. She goes a step further by saying it is deceptive and cruel to pretend or claim that someone can belong to God and be homosexual.

Some Christians believe it is loving to demand denial of homosexuality, ending relationships, changing to heterosexuality, or remaining celibate in order that the soul be saved. Others believe that sexual orientation is God-given, cannot be changed, and that it is cruel and unloving to demand it.

> "There is no valid evidence showing that sexual orientation can be changed."[4]
> —U.S. Surgeon General David Satcher, 2001

"As I heard more stories and evaluated my own reali-
ties, I realized change in orientation was not possible or
happening."[5]
—ALAN CHAMBERS, EXODUS INTERNATIONAL PRESIDENT,
2001–2013

In 2013, Chambers apologized to the LGBT community
for the "pain and hurt" Exodus had caused and announced
that the ministry was permanently shutting down. "Exodus
is an institution in the conservative Christian world, but
we've ceased to be a living, breathing organism. For quite
some time, we've been imprisoned in a worldview that's neither honoring toward our fellow human beings, nor biblical."

"Many interventions aimed at changing sexual orientation
have succeeded only in reducing or eliminating homosexual behavior rather than in creating or increasing
heterosexual attractions. They have, in effect, deprived
individuals of their capacity for sexual response to others.
These 'therapies' have often exposed their victims to electric shock or nausea-producing drugs while showing them
pictures of same-sex nudes (such techniques appear to be
less common today than in the past).

"Another problem in many published reports of 'successful' conversion therapies is that the participants'
initial sexual orientation was never adequately assessed.
Many bisexuals have been mislabeled as homosexuals
with the consequence that the 'successes' reported for the
conversions actually have occurred among bisexuals who

were highly motivated to adopt a heterosexual behavior pattern."

—APA Task Force on Appropriate Therapeutic Responses to Sexual Orientation, 2009

Threats of Hell and Loss

Those who do not deny their homosexuality, or end their relationships, or "change" to heterosexuality, or choose celibacy are threatened with Hell and rejection. Some Christians do not see it as making threats, but lovingly sharing the reality of God and His Word. Again, it comes down to the interpretation of the seven Scriptures cited to condemn homosexuals. No room is given for agreeing to disagree on interpretation. Gays and lesbians are forced into a dichotomy. They can deny their homosexuality, attempt to change something they cannot, struggle, pray, participate in reparative therapy or exorcism, or risk losing their families and church communities. Some may themselves interpret the Scriptures as condemning and may live in fear of losing their salvation.

The pain experienced in this scenario is excruciating. Another reason why I am writing this book. How do we move away from such harsh demands to more compassionate treatment? Take another look at the seven Scriptures? Read up on sexual orientation? Decide to "err" on the side of grace and love, and not make such harmful demands? Yes. Additionally, look at a list of abominations and realize that family and church members are not held to the same degree of condemnation for other sins as is reserved for homosexuality.

Abomination: *noun* – a thing that causes disgust or hatred

– a feeling of hatred (*Merriam-Webster*)

Little wonder that referring to homosexuals and homosexuality as abominations evokes such virulently strong emotions. Some will cite Leviticus 18:22 (KJV): "Thou shalt not lie with mankind, as with womankind: it is abomination," as though it grants Christians the right to use the term to label gays and lesbians, homosexuality, and same-sex marriage.

My question is, "WHY?" Why the need or willingness to use the label amid so many other Scriptures that talk about God's love, grace, kindness, and acceptance? Even if the seven Scriptures are interpreted as condemning of homosexuals (see Chapter 4 critique), why is that word so readily used to label? How could the use of the word by *loving* Christians not be damaging and hurtful? Why is the term not bandied around for other behaviors that are listed as abominations or sins in the Bible?

Ephesians 5:3–5 (KJV): But fornication, and all uncleanness, or covetousness, let it not be once named among you, as becometh saints; neither filthiness, nor foolish talking, nor jesting, which are not convenient: but rather giving of thanks. For this ye know, that no whoremonger, nor unclean person, nor covetous man, who is an idolater, hath any inheritance in the kingdom of Christ and God.

Galatians 5:21 (KJV): Now the works of the flesh are manifest, which are these; Adultery, fornication, uncleanness, lasciviousness, idolatry, witchcraft, hatred, variance, emulations, wrath, strife, seditions, heresies, envyings, murders, drunkenness, revellings, and such like: of the which I tell you before, as I have told you in time past, that they which do such things shall not inherit the kingdom of God.

I Corinthians 6:9–10 (KJV): Know ye not that the unrighteous shall not inherit the kingdom of God? Be not deceived: neither fornicators, nor idolaters, nor adulterers, nor effeminate, nor abusers of themselves with mankind, nor thieves, nor covetous, nor drunkards, nor revilers, nor extortioners, shall inherit the kingdom of God.

Sins that prevent one from entering the Kingdom of God: stealing, lying, fornication, adultery, slander, gluttony, lust, greed, pride, anger, envy, hatred, drunkenness. All these are preached about and against, but not with the vehemence reserved for homosexuality. Even with daily confession and repentance, we as humans do not steer clear of all items on the list. Yet we are not threatened with Hell.

Condemnation and demands that homosexuals change are based on seven Scriptures. As the Scriptures thought to promote slavery were eventually challenged, so should the Scriptures thought to condemn homosexuals.

The word "abomination" appears 152 times in the *New King James Version* of the Bible and seventy-four times in the *King James Version*. The number of times abomination is translated from the original Greek or Hebrew varies among translations, with only fifteen appearances in the *New English Translation*. There is no agreement among Christians on the use of the word itself in the Bible. Abomination appears the majority of the time in the Old Testament, and most often refers to pagan rituals, idolatry, unkosher foods, and unclean bodily practices. <u>It is used one time in reference to what is *perceived* as homosexuality—in Leviticus 18:22. Yet, that one reference to abomination is used as justification to label and condemn homosexuals.</u>

Those who add homosexuality to the list of sins mentioned in the New Testament often rank it at the top. There is no scriptural basis for rank-ordering sin. At the very least, homosexuals should be treated the same as those who lie, are envious, or are proud. The demands placed upon them by well-meaning church and family members is unjust and damaging.

Personal Cost

Those Who Surrender to the Demands Pay a Price

1. Deny their homosexuality

Some are asked to admit right up front that they are not really homosexual. They are expected to remain silent about it, act as though "it" never happened (attractions, relationships), admit it was a phase or temporary misjudgment, and begin acting as though they are heterosexual. They are required to lie about themselves.

2. End their love relationship

In order to remain in good standing with the Church and family, demands are made to end the relationship, to stay away from the loved one, and, depending upon the age, be subjected to surveillance. In addition to confusion and humiliation, the relationship itself is lost and grieved.

3. Change their sexual orientation

Some undergo reparative therapy, counseling, or exorcism to rid themselves of homosexuality. There are too many accounts of turmoil, struggle, confusion, self-loathing, and depression in attempts to change to heterosexuality. The expected visible proof of that "change" is dating or marrying the opposite sex.

4. Become celibate

If all else fails, homosexuals are expected to live a life of celibacy. Asking that of anyone is cruel. Some may take on celibacy as an honor, or see it as part of their devotion to God. If it is voluntary, it should obviously be respected. Most do not willingly choose a life without sexual expression and supportive companionship.

Those Who <u>Ignore the Demands</u> Pay a Price

Those who come out to family and church members who believe homosexuality is a sin, but choose not to adhere to their demands, risk condemnation, rejection, and excommunication. Some are kicked out of their homes, others are kicked out of their Churches. The subsequent pain and loss may lead to substance abuse, depression, and suicide. According to the Center for Disease Control and Prevention, depression affects LGBT people at higher rates than the heterosexual population, and that LGBT youths are more likely to report high levels of drug use and feelings of depression than heterosexual ones. LGBT youths in grades seven to twelve are twice as likely to attempt suicide than their heterosexual peers (CDC, 2016).[6]

Nathan Mathis, an Alabama farmer, drew extensive media coverage in December 2017 when he appeared at a political rally with a poster of his twenty-two-year-old lesbian daughter who had committed suicide. His remarks on video were viewed nearly three million times online.

> "I was antigay myself. I said bad things to my daughter myself, which I regret. How is my daughter a pervert just because she is gay?"[7]

He said he grew up in a Church where the preachers taught that homosexuality was wrong. "I heard that from the pulpit. And seeing real life like it really is, I realized how wrong I was… I told my daughter that I would rather my child was dead than to have a gay child." The discovery of Patti Sue's body, his daughter, marked the end of a family cycle of rejection, acceptance, and, finally, ultimate loss, Mathis said.

The personal cost to gays and lesbians in anti-homosexual families and Churches is exceptionally high. In order to remain safe, stay in churches, and not be condemned or rejected, many do not disclose their homosexuality and relationships.

Fannie's Story

My dear friend, Fannie Beynon, lived a long and full life. An intelligent, funny, hardworking, devout Christian with the brightest blue eyes, she recently passed away at ninety-one and left a legacy of a life well lived. I loved her dearly and dedicated this book to her.

Fannie was excited to hear that I was writing this book. She prayed, encouraged me, and wished she could have read a book like this when she was younger. Her enthusiasm was dampened several months before her passing, when a long-time Christian friend warned her that the Catholic Church would not approve of her name on the dedication page.

Fannie and Shirley, her partner of fifty-one years, loved the Church. They identified as Christians, as Catholics, but not as "out" lesbians. When I moved in across the street, they first introduced themselves as sisters. Years later, they began telling me stories of their love, how they met, their years in the Marine Corp, a forty-year career in nursing for Fannie and bookkeeping for Shirley. Except for the years they lived in San Francisco, they were closeted. Fannie married a gay man before meeting Shirley. She wore a wedding band and would point to it over the years to signify that she had been married to a man. They were married in name only for a short while, in order to avert threats at work.

I was with Fannie when news of the 2015 Supreme Court decision broke. She had been opposed to gay marriage, saying that it was unreasonable to advocate for it, that homosexuals did not have to "show their business" to everyone. She and Shirley had lived a quiet life and never "felt the need to draw attention to themselves." It is understandable that they internalized the expectations of family and Christian friends who were opposed to homosexuality. Neither of them recall anyone making direct demands. They were adamant that it was their choice not to reveal that they were gay and to live as "sisters."

However, with the Supreme Court ruling, Fannie changed her mind. Seeing that it was now possible for homosexuals to marry, she wept tears of joy, *and* of sadness. She wanted to be clear that she had a happy and satisfying life with Shirley, who had since passed away. Would she have married if she could have? Yes, and no. In a different time and place, but it would still not be possible to marry and stay in the Catholic Church.

In fact, friends at her Church had stepped up their antigay comments after the Supreme Court ruling. She wasn't sure it was directed at her, but she began to worry. She talked less about Shirley and no longer saw herself as gay in our last few conversations. Fannie was still actively involved in volunteer work in her last year. She sat in the hospital with dying patients who had no family, reading to them and praying.

Hers was a life of service and a close walk with God. A woman of deep faith who, at the end of her life, went further into the closet, denying her homosexuality and her relationship with the love of her life.

This chapter is titled Why It Matters. Fannie's story matters. The pain and the fallout of calling homosexuality an abomination; demanding denial, change or celibacy; rejection, excommunication, threats of hell—all matter. Regardless of how sincere or heartfelt the beliefs and demands of Christians, the damage runs deep and is often insurmountable. The alternative for many has been to remain closeted, even to marry the opposite sex as cover, to lie about themselves, and hide. Lesbian writer and activist Suzanne Pharr described her struggle:

"My life could not be shared with my family which in turn necessitated superficial relationships. The stress of maintaining vigilance over the lies I had to create for safety made me never able to relax. Perhaps worst of all was the damage to my sense of self, my sense of integrity. As a woman who had grown up deeply rooted in the church, albeit in tormented debate with it, and as a Southerner with deeply held and mostly unexamined values of courage and honesty, I had to view myself as a woman who lied because of fear."[8]

Deeply held, deeply rooted beliefs around integrity and being true to oneself as a homosexual. *Deeply held, deeply rooted* beliefs around homosexuality as sin. So much damage, so much pain. How do we get beyond this dichotomy, the judgment, the polarizing stances?

My final chapter asks readers to revisit Chapter 4, about

the Bible verses that are used to denounce homosexuality. If you are still convinced that the seven Scriptures condemn homosexuals, then reread Chapter 5, on what we now know about sexual orientation. If still convinced that sexual orientation does not exist and everyone is or should be heterosexual, look again at Chapter 6 and the stereotypes that have been used to inaccurately depict homosexuals. Challenge yourself or others who may use these stereotypes. Chapter 8 gives arguments for and against gay marriage. If still convinced that homosexuals should not be allowed to marry, ask yourself how you would feel if denied the right to marry the one you love based on someone else's religious beliefs.

What does the Bible say about how we should treat those we disagree with or who we believe are going to Hell? Chapter 11 offers strategies and solutions on how to bridge the divide between Christians and gays—how to promote healing and not to inflict more pain.

CHAPTER 11

WHAT CAN WE DO?

1. Read the Seven Scriptures

The Bible says very little about homosexuality. The relevant passages address exploitive forms of homoerotic sexual practices. The Holiness Codes of Leviticus 18:22 and 20:13 seek to preserve the male "seed" for propagation and survival. Romans 1:26–27 condemns men and women who violate sexual gender roles, male prostitution, and pederasty. In I Corinthians 6:9–10 and I Timothy 1:9–10, the translations of the Greeks words *malakoi* and *arsenokoitai* are varied. Most translations reference male prostitution and pederasty. Jude wrote about the sin of Sodom and Gomorrah: gang rape, inhospitality, and sex with angels (strange flesh).

None of the four Gospels report that Jesus said anything about homosexuality. This does not necessarily mean that

He had no opinion on the subject. But it is fair to suggest that neither He nor the authors of the Gospels considered it a very important concern. Yet seven Scriptures in the Bible are consistently used to condemn homosexuals—out of 31,102 verses. There are countless references to other sins, such as lying, stealing, coveting, love of money, gluttony, greed.

I respect my readers and understand that many will get to this point in the book firmly believing that those seven Scriptures condemn homosexuals. If that is the case, at the very least do not place homosexuality at the top of a list of sins. Christians are not expelled from Churches for lying, cheating, or greed. Some will argue that if members consistently participate in a sin, they might be asked to leave a Church. Granted, but not to the extent homosexuals are rejected by their Churches and Christian families.

Why should our attitudes change now, when for hundreds of years, homosexuality has been disparaged by religious authorities? A similar question was asked over a century ago about the Bible, slavery, and religious authority. Many began to question the interpretation of the Scriptures that were used to support slavery; now the Scriptures utilized to condemn homosexuality. New information and thinking came to light about natural law, human rights, and dignity. Christians could no longer justify owning slaves. New information about sexual orientation, emotional and physical attraction, and identity has come to light after over a century of research. It is my hope that Christians will no longer justify condemning homosexuals.

2. Look at Sexual Orientation

What is the cause of homosexuality? Is it a choice? Can it be changed? The answer to these questions hinges on an understanding of sexual orientation.

There is no consensus among scientists and psychologists as to what causes sexual orientation. We do not know why people are heterosexual, bisexual, or homosexual. More than a hundred theories have been proposed by scientists, psychologists, and religious leaders. There is a wide range of theories that try to explain the cause of homosexuality: biology, genetics, sex hormones, upbringing, mothers, fathers, siblings, birth order, Satan, God, sin, deception, peer pressure, disco music, bad marriages, mental illness, immaturity. The list goes on. No single scientific or religious theory fits all the evidence or holds up under the rigors of peer review by other researchers.

In all this confusion and disagreement among experts and religious leaders, there are many Christians who believe that they have a full understanding of sexual orientation, enough so to condemn homosexuals—a belief that sexual orientation does not exist and that anything but heterosexuality is a deviance.

"The first step to repentance is recognizing sin for what it is and rejecting deceptive attempts to sanitize it by calling it something else, i.e. 'choice,' 'sexual orientation,' 'she's not my wife, but we're soul mates,' and the like."[1]

—MATT BARBER

My question: do you have enough information or expertise to definitively decide that sexual orientation does not exist and you know the cause of homosexuality? Enough to condemn your homosexual friends, family, or church members? Enough to demand that they change or become celibate?

Albert Mohler, president of the Southern Baptist Theological Seminary, stated, "Early in this controversy, I felt it quite necessary, in order to make clear of the Gospel, to deny anything like a sexual orientation." He said he got it "wrong." "I repent of that." He went on to explain, "I believe that a biblical theological understanding, a robust biblical theology, would point to us that human sexual affective profiles—that who we are sexually—is far more deeply rooted than just the 'will'—if that were so easy." But Mohler went on to address revisionists who do not believe that the Bible condemns homosexuality. "If the revisionist arguments are right, then we've got to join them. I don't believe for a minute they are right."[2]

An acknowledgement that sexual orientation might exist beyond choice or will, but according to Mohler, homosexuality as an orientation is still a sin. Those who believe it is sin call for repentance and a change to heterosexuality.

3. Reevaluate Reparative Therapy

Conversion Therapy and LGBT Youth
Executive Summary of the Williams Institute
UCLA School of Law
January 2018

"An estimated 698,000 LGBT adults in the U.S. have received conversion therapy either from a licensed professional or a religious advisor or from both at some point in their lives, including about 350,000 LGBT adults who received conversion therapy as adolescents.

"Conversion therapy is treatment grounded in the belief that being LGBT is abnormal. It is intended to change the sexual orientation, gender identity, or gender expression of LGBT people. Conversion therapy is practiced by some licensed professionals in the context of providing health care and by some clergy or other spiritual advisors in the context of religious practice. Efforts to change someone's sexual orientation or gender identity are associated with poor mental health, including suicidality. To date, nine states, the District of Columbia, and 32 localities have banned health care professionals from using conversion therapy on youth.

"Exclusions for therapy provided by religious or spiritual advisors leave many youth vulnerable to conversion counseling even in states with bans. An estimated 57,000 youth (ages 13–17) across all states will receive conversion therapy from religious or spiritual advisors before they reach the age of 18."[3]

In all fairness, there are those who have gone through conversion therapy and believe that their orientation was changed. It is important to note that those individuals were adults who felt they were not forced into therapy. However, these stories are in the minority. There are so many more stories of gays and lesbians who have gone through conversion therapy that tell of being suicidal, humiliated, alienated from their families during therapy, bullied, and threatened with condemnation and expulsion from their Churches. They were described as sick, sinful, lustful abominations and set up for expectations that they could not meet. Try as they may, they could not change their orientation.

> "I was 9 years old when I recognized my attractions for the same gender. Praying to God every night and pleading with Him to take my feelings away didn't work. Practically living, eating, and breathing the Bible didn't work. I tried repressing and denying who I was—but nothing changed inside of me. I was taught by my pastors, parents and peers to hate myself—and *that* worked."
>
> —ANONYMOUS

4. Challenge Stereotypes

Homosexuals have been characterized as evil, sinful, unnatural, promiscuous, having an agenda, perverted, molesters, and recruiters. All of these are stereotypes that no one would want to be on the receiving end of—all are polarizing labels. Labels that harm, that dehumanize, and point to a group of people as less than. A few highlights below from what I have written in Chapter 6 call for compassion and a rethinking of stereotypes that have been used.

> "It is unfortunate that something someone disagrees with, doesn't understand, or can't relate to, is then deemed *unnatural.*"

"If *gays could recruit*, then heterosexuals could also. That ironically is the basis for reparative therapy—heterosexual recruitment or therapizing. Again, there is no proof of the effectiveness of reparative therapy. There are countless testimonies to the contrary and to subsequent damage."

"A *homosexual agenda* implies that gays recruit, are out to destroy Christianity, and are plotting to take over the American economy and society. Gays cannot recruit any more than heterosexuals can. "Christianity is not at risk of being annihilated with Christians accounting for 72% of the U.S. population, and a 5 to 10% gay population is not large enough to dominate politically or economically."

Stereotyping is as common as the air we breathe. Engaging in critical thinking, being self-aware, looking at why we believe what we believe about someone different than ourselves are all essential to countering stereotypes. The goal is to prevent stereotypes in the first place or, at the very least, question and understand how they develop. It is also important to understand the damaging effects of stereotypes and the negative impact they have on those who are targeted.

5. Agree to Disagree on Gay Marriage

The concerted effort through courts, legislations, businesses, and Churches to end gay marriage, to condemn it, to refuse to recognize it or participate in it negatively impacts gays and lesbians. Weddings signify joy, celebration, family, community, and commitment. All are positive attributes ignored or still considered sinful or unholy based on the biblical interpretation of conservative Christians.

What would the outcome be for homosexuals if Christians were successful in making same-sex marriage illegal? Gay couples and their children would be devastated to be stripped of legal recognition and rights. To be honest, I find it perplexing that loving and sincere Christians want to revoke a right that they themselves enjoy. Overturning *Obergefell v Hodges* would be the first time in our nation's history that a Supreme Court decision would revoke rights it previously granted and had determined were constitutional.

We all have the right to our own religious beliefs, to associate, to marry accordingly. But someone else's religious beliefs should not determine who any of us have the right to marry. Religion or being religious is not a legal requirement for marriage in the United States. Religions do not determine who has the right to marry in a democracy. None of us would want to be denied the right to marry the person we love because of someone else's religious beliefs.

6. Recognize the Pain Inflicted

When individuals believe, and the Churches preach, that homosexuality is an abomination, it is painful. When an entire demographic is targeted as going to Hell, in need of redemption, and are required to "change" their sexual orientation in order to be accepted and remain in good standing, it is damaging. It matters to those who have lost their families, communities, and Churches, to those who have been subjected to conversion therapy, required to remain celibate, or to deny their sexual orientation. It also matters to the friends, family, ministers, and church members of those gays and lesbians who have been condemned and rejected.

Little wonder that there is such a divide in our society and in our Churches. How do God-fearing, sincere, Bible-believing Christians shore up their interpretation of Scriptures with everyday encounters with gays and lesbians? So many are torn between their love for someone who is gay and accepting or welcoming them, in the face of their own strongly-held beliefs against homosexuality. These inner and outer conflicts play out in families, congregations, and society as a whole.

7. Contribute to the Healing

"Be always humble, gentle, and patient. Show your love by being tolerant with one another. Do your best to preserve unity which the Spirit gives by means of the peace that binds you together"

EPHESIANS 4:2–3 (GNT).

"My children, our love should not be just words and talk; it must be true love, which shows itself in action"

1 JOHN 3:18 (GNT).

"Above everything, love one another earnestly, because love covers over many sins"

1 PETER 4:8 (NIV).

"And now I give you a new commandment: love one another. As I have loved you, so you must love one another"

JOHN 13:34 (NIV).

"Do not judge, or you too will be judged. For in the same way you judge others, you will be judged, and with the measure you use, it will be measured to you"

MATTHEW 7:1–2 (NIV).

"Do not judge, and you will not be judged. Do not condemn, and you will not be condemned. Forgive, and you will be forgiven"

LUKE 6:37 (NIV).

"Be merciful, just as your Father is merciful"

LUKE 6:36 (NIV).

Some Christians believe that it is loving to demand denial of homosexuality, ending relationships, changing to heterosexuality, or remaining celibate, in order that the soul be saved. Others believe that sexual orientation is God-given, cannot be changed, and that it is cruel and unjust to demand it.

Some Christians do not see it as making threats, but

lovingly sharing the reality of God and His Word. Again, it comes down to the interpretation of the seven Scriptures cited to condemn homosexuals. No room is given for agreeing to disagree on interpretation.

The demands and condemnation placed upon gays and lesbians by well-meaning Church and family members is unjust and damaging. Let's move away from such harshness and into more compassionate treatment—help to heal, not inflict pain.

INTERPRETATION OF SCRIPTURES

Seven Scriptures are used to denounce homosexuals. Seven Scriptures cited above speak of love, mercy, humility, being tolerant, and not judging. There are countless more that emphasize the same—from Jesus, Paul, Peter, and John.

What do we do with the seven Scriptures that "condemn" homosexuals when so many other Scriptures call for mercy, love, and acceptance? Many will say that not standing firm against homosexuality is winking at sin, nodding at the Devil, embracing the ways of the world, compromising God's Word and will.

But what if there is enough disagreement on the "sin" of homosexuality? What if condemning homosexuals and requiring they change to heterosexuality is *compromising* God's Word? There is little disagreement on most sins—lying, cheating, greed, pride. And there are so many more Scriptures devoted to these sins. Can we base such condemnation, harmful demands, and even loathing on seven Scriptures in light of what we now know about sexual orientation and conversion therapy?

I am not asking for a suspension of belief or commitment to the Bible. I am asking that we reconsider the seven Scriptures for the sake of gays and lesbians who have been hurt, who find themselves locked into despair when they cannot change their orientation. Or as celibates, they are denied a lifetime of intimacy. Or they are kicked out of their families and Churches.

Those who changed their minds on the interpretation of Scriptures used to support slavery were accused of being weak and compromising. Their faith and salvation were questioned. Some said you could not be Christian and disagree over the Scriptures that "clearly" condoned and called for slavery. Lines were drawn between Churches and denominations.

Slaves adapted Christianity and the Word of God to include themselves—simultaneous interpretations of the same Bible. One interpretation saw slavery as natural and of God's will, the other saw God's grace and the promise of freedom. It is clear evidence that multiple biblical interpretations can and do coexist.

THE CHURCH'S ROLE

"A debate over homosexual marriage would only be possible in a society that has already cast off moral restraint.

Most professing Christians in this world talk about loving God, but they ignore what he says and excuse homosexuals. In fact, some are homosexuals themselves."

"You can see our families are falling apart, our nation is falling apart, our churches are falling apart. The homosexual lifestyle can never produce happiness. Because of all this, God says, 'I will not spare you.' Better change or pay the price."[4]

—PASTOR (*MUSCATINE JOURNAL*,
LETTER TO EDITOR, 2010)

This letter was written by an Iowa minister in my hometown, but could have been written by any number of ministers throughout the United States. Strong beliefs, strong sentiments expressed about lacking *moral restraint* if even discussing homosexuality. *Excusing* homosexuals in the face of what God says. Families, country, and Churches *falling apart*. Change or pay the *price*, meaning homosexuals, as well as those who *accept* them.

Here lies the dilemma. Not that any reader has gotten to this point in the book without wondering, but how do we handle this in our Churches? How should we treat gays and lesbians in our midst? This pastor offers little choice. He has "thrown down the gauntlet," so to speak. End of discussion. It's my (God's) way or the highway. All too familiar—and many pastors and congregants would agree with him. So where does that leave us? As Christians who look to the Bible for guidance? As Christians who look to Jesus as an example of the life we want to lead?

What would Jesus do? He didn't say anything about homosexuality. He had much to say about mercy, love, kindness, and compassion. What would God do? "Christians in this world talk about loving God, but they ignore what he says, and excuse homosexuals." "God says I will not spare you." This Iowa minister interpreted the seven Scriptures as a condemnation of homosexuals, and said that *God says* they should not be excused and that they will not be spared.

What about Christians in this pastor's congregation who aren't sure of the Scriptures used to attack homosexuals? Who aren't sure what causes homosexuality and whether or not it can be changed? Who aren't sure that gays and lesbians in their families or congregations should be condemned, forced to change, or kicked out?

The first place homosexuals should be able to turn to is the Church. Sadly, it is often the last. Many Churches either condemn them or remain silent and embarrassed over an issue that has caused much division and despair. Too often, the voices and lives of those affected go unnoticed as rules and policies about homosexuality are debated.

Ministers across the nation find themselves in a difficult position. They may believe that Scriptures condemn homosexuality, but also believe that all congregants should be loved, accepted, and respected, including homosexuals. The Nashville Statement, recently signed by 160 ministers, declared that not only is homosexuality a sin, "*approval* of homosexual immorality" is also. This puts Christians who may have accepted homosexual family, friends, or congregants on notice, if that acceptance or love is seen as *approval*.

Those ministers or church members who provide safety and comfort instead of making painful demands risk being accused of promoting or advocating homosexuality. Their own salvation may be questioned. Too often, there is little room for disagreement in Churches, without judging or calling into question someone's faith or salvation. Ministers and other Church leaders can effectively address this divide.

Talk About It

Ministers can study the seven Scriptures with congregants. They can establish their Church doctrine on homosexuality, their own interpretation of the Scriptures, and open it up for discussion. Use this book, refer to Chapter 4. Use texts from your own denomination, along with those that offer opposing viewpoints. Look at the doctrines of a variety of Churches in Chapter 7. There is no harm in talking about it. Discussion and study may confirm what church members already believe. They are now familiar with the Scriptures being used to condemn homosexuality, and they also understand how others may interpret those Scriptures differently.

Establish guidelines for civil dialogue. How to disagree without personal attacks, how to refrain from negatively labelling those in disagreement, how to provide an environment of safety and respect. Most Church leaders are experienced in navigating these kinds of difficult discussions, but may not be comfortable with the topic of homosexuality.

Consultants and educators like myself can provide training on Christianity and homosexuality, as well as civil discourse for Church groups.

Don't Demonize Homosexuals

In the course of preaching heartfelt and scriptural beliefs, some ministers have villainized homosexuality, and have perpetuated myths and stereotypes about homosexuals. Be familiar with these negative stereotypes, don't let them go unchallenged, and, at the very least, don't reinforce them.

Call for Compassion

Pope Francis responded to a question about homosexuality:

"A person once asked me, in a provocative manner, if I approved of homosexuality. I replied with another question, 'Tell me: when God looks at a gay person, does He endorse the existence of this person with love, or reject and condemn this person?' We must always consider the person. Here we enter into the mystery of the human being. In life, God accompanies persons, and we must accompany them, starting from their situation. It is necessary to accompany them with mercy. When that happens, the Holy Spirit inspires the priest to say the right thing.[5]

"If a person is gay and seeks God and has good will,

who am I to judge him? The Catechism of the Catholic Church explains this very well. It says they should not be marginalized because of this (orientation) but that they must be integrated into society. The problem is not having this orientation. We must be brothers."[6]

Leave Judgment to God

I am fortunate that my father modelled this for me at the end of his life. I remember so fondly that day, when my seventy-eight-year-old father, a conservative minister, asked that I forgive him for judging me. His beliefs and interpretation of the Bible remained intact. But he did not want to come down on the wrong side of judgment, or as judging. Thankfully, he shared that with me while he was still alive.

I know that I am blessed to have had that kind of relationship with my father. I am also fortunate that I have had a loving, personal relationship with God. I didn't struggle or take on the disapproval and condemnation I received from my father and others over the years. It was a condemnation that was well-meaning and expressed in love, but nonetheless a condemnation.

It is a double-edged sword—love and condemnation.

We Love You, But You're Going to Hell
or instead
We Love You...

About the Author

Dr. Kim O'Reilly is an expert in the field of intercultural and cross-cultural understanding and communication. She is the founder and principal of Intercultural Solutions, a training and consulting firm dedicated to preparing businesses, community leaders, and educators with knowledge and strategies to address cultural differences in the workplace.

A professor of Cultural Studies and Teacher Education for the last seventeen years, she is recognized for her commitment to promoting understanding, respect, and appreciation of other cultures without heavy-handedness or finger-pointing. Dr. O'Reilly has earned accolades from students and faculty, including the Excellence in Teaching Nomination and the Senior Scholar Faculty Mentor Award.

The work of "Building Bridges Across Cultures" has taken her to Germany, as a member of the U.S. Education Delegation to the University of Hamburg, where she partnered with German educators to redesign Holocaust education in German schools. She was also selected for the Northern Ireland Peace and Conflict Delegation, where she worked with Irish educators to develop new curriculum policy for Irish students.

She speaks, writes articles, and delivers transformative training that brings people together to bridge racial, religious, ethnic, sexual orientation, and gender differences. She creates a safe space for participants to share their own viewpoints and to gain a deeper understanding of others'.

For more information on her training and consulting programs in Diversity and Inclusion, Anti-Bullying and Conflict Resolution, Cultural Competence, and Multicultural Education, please visit her Web site: https://www.interculturalsolutions.net/.

Notes

Chapter 1. Introduction

1. Scott Rutherford, "Duck Dynasty: Union Thought Police Want Phil Robertson Fans Fired," *Inquisitr*, June 13, 2014, http://www.inquisitr.com/1297660/duck-dynasty-union-thought-police.
2. Rutherford, "Union Thought Police."
3. Billy Hallowell, "Duck Dynasty Star Phil Robertson Speaks Out About 'Common Sense' and Sin After Outrage Over His Homosexuality Comments," *The Blaze*, December 23, 2013, http://www.theblaze.com/stories/2013/12/23/.

Chapter 2. My Story

1. Jack Hyles, *Two Messages by Dr. Jack Hyles* (Hammond, IN: Hyles Publications, 1969), 9-15.

Chapter 3. Scriptures Used to Promote Slavery and Segregation

1. Jefferson Davis, "Inaugural Address as Provisional President of the Confederacy," *Confederate States of America, Congressional Journal* 1 (1861): 64-66.

2. Alexander Campbell, *The Christian System* (Cincinnati: Standard Publishing, 1845), 204.

3. Josiah Priest, *Bible Defence of Slavery: And Origin, Fortunes, and History of the Negro Race* (Louisville, KY: J.F. Brennan Publishing, 1851).

4. *Scott v State*, (39 GA 321, Quoted in Ref. 1, 1869).

5. Fay Botham, *Almighty God Created the Races: Christianity, Interracial Marriage, and American Law* (University of North Carolina Press, 2013).

Chapter 4. Scriptures Used to Condemn Homosexuals

1. Michael Avioz, "Josephus's Portrayal of Lot and His Family," *Journal for the Study of the Pseudepigrapha,* 16.1 (2006): 7-8.

2. Troy D. Perry, *Don't Be Afraid Anymore: The Story of Reverend Troy Perry and the Metropolitan Community Churches* (New York: St. Martin's Press, 1992), 342.

3. Perry, *Don't Be Afraid Anymore*, 343.

4. David Gushee, "Two Odd Little Words: The LGBT Issue, Part 11 (Revised)," *Baptist News Global,* September 19, 2014, 2, https://www.baptistnews.com.

5. Gushee, "Two Odd Little Words," 3-4.

6. Patrick M. Chapman, *Thou Shalt Not Love: What Evangelicals Really Say to Gays* (Bayonne, NJ: Haiduk Press, 2008), 124-125.

Chapter 5. Sexual Orientation

1. "Lesbian, Gay, Bisexual, Transgender," American Psychological Association, accessed July 19, 2018, https://www.apa.org/Topics.

2. Christy Mallory, Taylor N.T. Brown and Kerith J. Conron, "Conversion Therapy and LGBT Youth," The Williams

Institute: UCLA School of Law, January 2018, 1, https://www.williamsinstitute.law.ucla.edu.

3. "Just the Facts about Sexual Orientation & Youth: A Primer for Principals, Educators, & School Personnel," American Psychological Association, accessed July 19, 2018, https://www.apa.org/pi/lgbt/resources/just-the-facts.pdf, 3.

4. APA, "Just the Facts," 3.

5. APA, "Just the Facts," 3.

6. APA, "Just the Facts," 3.

7. APA, "Just the Facts," 3.

8. APA, "Just the Facts," 4.

9. Elise Schmelzer, "Five Christian Pastors in Illinois Are Challenging a State Law Banning 'Conversion Therapy' for Gay Youth," *Washington Post*, August 12, 2016.

10. Wayne Besen, "Love In Action Co-Founder: My Ministry Shatters Lives," *Ex-Gay Watch*, July 30, 2005, http://www.exgaywatch.com.

11. David Roberts, "Former Love In Action Director John Smid Offers Apology," *Ex-Gay Watch*, March 4, 2010, http://www.exgaywatch.com.

12. John Paulk, "To Straight and Back: My Life as an Ex-Ex-Gay Man," *Politico*, June 19, 2014, 5-6.

13. Alan Chambers, "I Once Led an Ex-Gay Ministry. Here's Why I Now Support People in Gay Marriages," *Washington Post*, June 26, 2015.

Chapter 6. Stereotypes and Myths

1. Daniel Reynolds, "Gallup Poll: A Record Number of Americans Identify as LGBT," *Advocate*, January 12, 2017.

2. "Early Diagnosis and Effective Treatment," Child Molestation Research and Prevention Institute, 2016, 1.

3. CMRPI, "Early Diagnosis," 2.

4. CMRPI, "Early Diagnosis," 9-10.

5. CMRPI, "Early Diagnosis," 11.

6. Ryan Anderson, "Nearly Everything the Media Tell You About Sexual Orientation and Gender Identity Is Wrong," *CNS News*, August 22, 2016, http://www.cnsnews.com.

7. John Paulk, "To Straight and Back: My Life as an Ex-Ex Gay Man," *Politico,* June 19, 2014, 1.

8. "Understanding Alcohol Use Disorders and Their Treatment," American Psychological Association, accessed July 19, 2018, https://www.apa.org.

9. Tara Wanda Merrigan, "Readers React to GQ's Duck Dynasty Story and Phil Robertson's Indefinite Suspension," *GQ*, December 19, 2013, 1.

10. "Homosexuality: Brief Quotations," Religious Tolerance, accessed August 20, 2017, 1, http://www.religious tolerance.org.

11. Star Parker, "Left's Homosexual Campaign: Not About Freedom, But Delegitimization and Annihilation of Christianity," *CNS News*, April 6, 2015, 1, http://www. cnsnews.com.

12. Jerry Falwell, Views on Homosexuality, Wikipedia, accessed July 19, 2018, https://en.wikipedia.org.

Chapter 7. Ministers and Churches

1. Jim Hill and Rand Cheadle, *The Bible Tells Me So* (New York: Anchor Books, 1996), 69-70.

2. "Homosexuality: Brief Quotations," Religious Tolerance, accessed August 2017, 2, http://www.religious tolerance.org.

3. Bruce Hilton, *Can Homophobia Be Cured? Wrestling with Questions that Challenge the Church* (Nashville: Abingdon Press, 1992), 40.

4. Paul Gebhart, "New River Media Interview with: Paul Gebhard," interview by Ben Wattenberg, *First Measured Century*, PBS, http://www.pbs.org/fmc/interviews/gebhard.html.

5. Tyler Austin, "Today in Gay History: Gay Activist Pies Anita Bryant in the Face," *Out*, October 14, 2016, 2.

6. Michael W. Chapman, "Billy Graham's Daughter: God Is Turning Away from America and Leaving Us to Our Sins," *CNS News*, April 26, 2016, 1, http://www.cnsnews.com.

7. Morgan Lee, "Franklin Graham Defends Comments on Gay Activists and Islam, Compares Himself to Father Speaking Out for MLK," *The Christian Post*, March 27, 2014, 1.

8. Michael W. Chapman, "Rev. Graham: I Won't Be Buying Girl Scout Cookies This Year," *CNS News*, March 1, 2016, 1, http://www.cnsnews.com.

9. Michael W. Chapman, "Franklin Graham on Changing His Views on Homosexuality: God Would Have to Shift, And God Doesn't," *CNS News*, January 8, 2014, 1, http://www.cnsnews.com.

10. Morgan Lee, "Franklin Graham Defends Comments on Gay Activists and Islam, Compares Himself to Father Speaking Out for MLK," *The Christian Post*, March 27, 2014, 2.

11. Chancellor Agard, "Duck Dynasty Ending: Phil Robertson's Controversial Quotes," *Entertainment*, November 17, 2016, 1.

12. "Sexuality," Position Statements, Southern Baptist Convention, accessed July 20, 2018, http://www.sbc.net.

13. "Watchtower View of Homosexuality and Transgenderism," Jehovah's Witnesses, accessed August 22, 2017, http://www.jwfacts.com/watchtower/homosexuality-gay-jehovahs-witnesses.php.

14. *Is Homosexuality a Sin?* (Washington, DC: Parent, Families, and Friends of Lesbians and Gays Publications, 1992), 8-11.

Chapter 8. Marriage

1. "Nashville Statement," CBMW: A Coalition for Biblical Sexuality, accessed July 20, 2018, Article 1, https://www.cbmw.org.
2. CBMW, "Nashville Statement," Preamble.
3. CBMW, "Nashville Statement," Article 10.
4. Michael Barbaro, "A Scramble as Biden Backs Same-Sex Marriage," *New York Times*, May 6, 2012, 2.
5. Curtis M. Wong, "Texas Congressman Wants to Put Gay People on an Island to See If They Die Out," *Huffpost Gay Voices*, November 4, 2015, 1.
6. Zack Ford, "No, Marco Rubio Did Not Just Preach Tolerance for LGBT People," *Think Progress*, August 15, 2016, 2.
7. Catherine Garcia, "Duck Dynasty's Phil Robertson Calls Gay Marriage 'Evil,' 'Sinful' During Ted Cruz Event," *The Week*, January 31, 2016, 1.
8. Meghan Keneally, "Ted Cruz Responds to Gay Man About Religious Freedom," ABC News, April 18, 2016, https://abcnews.go.com.
9. Judd Legum, "Rubio Outlines Plan to End Marriage Equality," *Think Progress*, December 13, 2015, 1.
10. Brian Brown, "The Federal Government Has the Right to Define Marriage," *U.S. News and World Report*, December 16, 2012, 1.
11. Jessica Taylor, "Cruz: Opposition to Same-Sex Marriage Will Be 'Front And Center' in 2016 Campaign," National Public Radio, Inc., transcript, June 29, 2015.
12. Ryan T. Anderson, "Marriage and the Constitution: What the Court Said and Why It Got It Wrong," *Real Clear Politics*, July 03, 2015, 1.
13. Marina Fang, "Rick Santorum Will Fight the Supreme Court If It Legalizes Gay Marriage," *The Huffington Post*, May 31, 2015, 1.

14. Curtis M. Wong, "SCOTUS's Gay Marriage Decision Is 'Unconstitutional' and 'Un-American,' According to Bryan Fischer," *The Huffington Post*, October 8, 2014, 1.
15. Steve Benen, "Cruz, Rubio Vow to Fight Against Marriage Equality," MSNBC, The Maddow Blog, December 4, 2015, 1.
16. David Edwards, "Grow a Spine!: Huckabee Explodes at GOP for Giving Up as Gays Break 'Nature's Law' of Marriage," *Raw Story*, October 13, 2014, 1.
17. Raw Story, "Grow a Spine," 2.
18. *Lambda Legal and Marriage Equality in Nevada* (New York: Lambda Legal Publications, August 17, 2012), 1-2.
19. Laura Myers, "Nevada GOP Drops Platforms Against Abortions, Gay Marriage, Endorses Sandoval," *Las Vegas Review-Journal*, April 12, 2014, 2.
20. Obergefell Et Al. v. Hodges, Director, Ohio Department of Health, Et Al., Certiorari to the United States Court of Appeals for the Sixth Circuit, Decided June 26, 2015, https://www.supremecourt.gov/opinions/14pdf/14-556_3204.pdf.
21. Jonathan Merritt, "Pastors Opposed to Gay Marriage Swear Off All Civil Ceremonies," *Salt Lake Tribune*, November 30, 2014, 1-2.
22. Zack Ford, "Republican Presidential Candidates Want You to Know They Are Against LGBT Rights," *Think Progress*, December 8, 2015, 2.
23. Phil Robertson, "We Stand with Phil Robertson – Boycott A&E" Facebook page, December 18, 2013, https://www.facebook.com/timelinephotos21of23.
24. Denny Burk, "The Southern Baptist Convention Passes Resolution on Gay Marriage," *Denny Burk: A Commentary on Theology, Politics, and Culture,* June 16, 2015, 1, http://www.dennyburk.com.
25. Denny Burk: A Commentary, "SBC Passes Resolution," 2.

26. "Traditional Marriage," Faith in America, accessed August 20, 2017, 2, http://www.faithinamerica.org.

27. Curtis M. Wong, "Here's Why Pat Robertson Insists That Gay Marriage Is Still Illegal," *Huffpost Gay Voices*, October 26, 2015, 1.

28. "Evangelical Initiative," Faith in America, accessed August 20, 2017, 1, http://www.faithinamerica.org.

29. Zack Ford, "Arkansas Catholic Schools Crack Down on LGBT Students," *Think Progress*, September 12, 2016, 3.

30. Gabrielle Banks, "Man Sues to Marry His Laptop in Protest of Same-Sex Rights," *Houston Chronicle*, April 15, 2016.

31. Jacob Kerr and Amanda Terkel, "Civil War and Endless Trauma: What Opponents Predict Will Happen If Marriage Equality Is Legalized," *Huffington Post*, June 17, 2015, 1.

32. Kerr and Terkel, "Civil War and Endless Trauma," 1.

33. Kerr and Terkel, "Civil War," 2.

34. Kerr and Terkel, "Civil War," 2.

35. Kerr and Terkel, "Civil War," 3.

36. Kerr and Terkel, "Civil War," 3.

37. John Piper, "Let Marriage Be Held in Honor: Thinking Biblically About So-Called Same-Sex Marriage," *Desiring God,* accessed August 20, 2017, https://www.desiringgod.org.

38. Jacob Kerr and Amanda Terkel, "Civil War and Endless Trauma: What Opponents Predict Will Happen If Marriage Equality Is Legalized," *Huffington Post*, June 17, 2015, 3.

39. Obergefell Et Al. v. Hodges, Director, Ohio Department of Health, Et Al., Certiorari to the United States Court of Appeals for the Sixth Circuit, Decided June 26, 2015, https://www.supremecourt.gov/opinions/14pdf/14-556_3204.pdf.

40. Fenton Johnson, "Wedded to an Illusion: Do Gays and Lesbians Really Have the Right to Marry?" *Harper's Magazine*, November 1996, 46.

Chapter 9. Religious Freedom

1. Marshall Zelinger, "You've Heard from the Baker. Now Hear from the Woman Called Out by the Supreme Court in Its Ruling," *9 News*, June 6, 2018, 1, http://www.9news.com.
2. Jack Phillips, "Supreme Court Decision Says My Faith Is Welcomed Back in America: Cake Artist Jack Phillips," *USA Today*, June 4, 2018.
3. Jack Phillips, "Supreme Court Decision."
4. Jack Phillips, "Supreme Court Decision."
5. Samuel Smith, "Supreme Court Rules Christian Baker Jack Phillips Can Refuse to Make Gay Wedding Cakes," *The Christian Post,* June 4, 2018.
6. "Masterpiece Case Explained and What Can You Do Now?" The Interfaith Alliance of Colorado newsletter, June 3, 2018, http://www.outreach@interfaithalliance.org.
7. Jenny Jarvie, "Mississippi Governor Signs Law That Allows Businesses to Refuse Service to Gay Couples," *Los Angeles Times*, April 5, 2016.
8. Stephanie Wang, "Judge to Hear Challenge to Indiana 'Religious Freedom' Fix," *The Indianapolis Star*, August 15, 2016.
9. Curtis M. Wong, "California Bakery Can Refuse to Make Cakes for Same-Sex Weddings, Judge Rules," *Huffington Post*, February 6, 2018.
10. David G. Savage, "Battles Over Religious Freedom Are Sure to Follow Same-Sex Marriage Ruling," *Los Angeles Times,* July, 13, 2015.
11. Savage, "Battles Over Religious Freedom."

Chapter 10. Why It Matters

1. Sejal Singh and Laura E. Durso, "Widespread Discrimination Continues to Shape LGBT People's Lives in Both Subtle and

Significant Ways," Center for American Progress, May 2, 2017, 1-7, https://americanprogress.org.
2. "2017 Workplace Equality Fact Sheet," Out and Equal, accessed July 19, 2018, http://www.outandequal.org.
3. Stoyan Zaimov, "Ex-Lesbian Talks Leaving Behind 'Super Wild' Lifestyle with Women, Turning to Jesus in Viral Video," *Christian Post*, January 2, 2018.
4. "Surgeon General's Report Urges Openness About Sexual Issues," *Associated Press*, June 29, 2001, accessed August 20, 2017, http://www.articles.latimes.com.
5. Jonathan Merritt, "The Downfall of the Ex-Gay Movement," *The Atlantic*, October 6, 2015.
6. "First National Study of Lesbian, Gay, and Bisexual High School Students' Health," Centers for Disease Control and Prevention, August 11, 2016, https://www.cdc.gov.
7. Heidi Stevens, "On 'Ellen,' A Father's Grief Over His Gay Daughter and A Call for Us All to Do Better," *Chicago Tribune*, December 19, 2017.
8. Suzanne Pharr, *Homophobia: A Weapon of Sexism* (Eureka Springs, AR: Women's Project, 1988), *xiv*.

Chapter 11. What Can We Do?

1. J. Matt Barber, "Embracing the False Gospel of Tolerance Instead of Christ's Grace," *CNS News*, May 2, 2016, http://www.cnsnews.com.
2. Zack Ford, "Three Days in Nashville Talking to Southern Baptists About Homosexuality," *Think Progress*, October 30, 2014, 3-4.
3. Christy Mallory, Taylor N.T. Brown and Kerith J. Conron, "Conversion Therapy and LGBT Youth," The Williams Institute: UCLA School of Law, January 2018, 1-3, https://williamsinstitute.law.ucla.edu.

4. Don Hoover, "Homosexuality is Destroying Nation," *The Muscatine Journal*, November 5, 2010, http://www.muscatinejournal.com/new/opinion/mailbag.

5. Antonio Spadaro, "A Big Heart Open to God: An Interview with Pope Francis," *American Magazine*, September 30, 2013, 20-21.

6. Vatican City, "'Who Am I to Judge?' Pope's Remarks Do Not Change Church Teaching," *Catholic Sentinel*, accessed July 22, 2018, 1, https://www.catholicsentinel.org.

.